FUTURE WORK

FUTURE
WORK

*Jobs, self-employment and leisure
after the industrial age*

JAMES ROBERTSON

Gower/Maurice Temple Smith

Published by

Gower Publishing Company Limited,
Gower House,
Croft Road,
Aldershot,
Hants GU11 3HR,
England

British Library Cataloguing in Publication Data

Robertson, James
  Future work : jobs, self-employment and leisure
  after the industrial age.
  1. Industrial sociology   2. Technology—Social
  aspects
  I. Title
  306'.36   HD6955

ISBN 0 85117 259 8 (hardback); 0 85117 2601 (paperback)
Typeset by BookEns, Saffron Walden, Essex
Printed and bound in Great Britain by
Biddles Ltd, Guildford and King's Lynn

Contents

Introduction   ix

PART 1: WHAT COMES AFTER THE EMPLOYMENT AGE?   1

Chapter 1.   Possible Futures for Work   3
             A Post-Industrial Age   3
             Two Visions of Post-Industrial Society   4
             Three Futures for Work   5
             Three Possible Futures   6
Chapter 2.   A Realistic Assessment   17
             The Four-Sector Economy   17
             Restoring Full Employment – A Realistic Goal?   20
             Leisure in Place of Work – A Realistic Goal?   24
             The Significance of Ownwork   26
Chapter 3.   The Age of Employment   28
             Pre-Industrial Patterns of Work   28
             The Situation Now   29
             Employment as Dependency   30
             Masculine, Impersonal Work   31
             Exclusive Nature of Employment   33
             Dependency of Local Communities   35
             Limits to Employment   38
Chapter 4.   A Change of Direction   39
             Energy   40
             Technology   41
             Environment   42
             Leisure   44
             Education and Training   47
             Incomes   48
             Capital, Investment, Land   50

PART 2: CHANGING PERCEPTIONS OF WORK   53

Chapter 5.   The Work Ethic Evolves   55
             The Protestant Reformation   56
             Attitudes to Time and Money   58

A Work Ethic for All   60
Change as Liberation and Progress   62
Work Ethic or Leisure Ethic?   63
A New Work Ethic   68
Chapter 6.   Changing Worldview, Changing Values   71
The Industrial-Age Outlook   71
A Post-Industrial Worldview   73
Shifting Values   76
Masculine and Feminine   79
Men's Work and Women's Work   81
Equal Opportunities   83
The Feminisation of Work   87
Chapter 7.   The Valuation of Work   89
The Theory of the Just Price   90
The Labour Theory of Value   91
The Neo-Classical Economists   97
The Supremacy of Quantitative Values   100
The Failure of Quantitative Evaluation   102
Pointers for the Future   105

PART 3: THE END OF THE EMPLOYMENT EMPIRE   107

Chapter 8.   Labour   109
Defensive Posture   110
The Lucas Initiative   113
Work Rights and Responsibilities   116
Depersonalisation   119
Transformation of the Working Class   121
Chapter 9.   Money   126
Money Now Dominant   126
Possibilities for the Future   128
Money and Ownwork   130
Positive and Negative Effects   133
A 'Dissolution of the Monasteries'?   135
Chapter 10.   Politics and Government   137
Political Alignments during the Industrial Age   137
Possible Futures for Politics and Government   138
A Scenario   141
Collapse or Decolonisation   144

PART 4: PRACTICALITIES OF THE TRANSITION   147

Chapter 11.   The Shift to Ownwork Has Already Begun   149
Personal Ownwork   150
Local Ownwork   152
Business and Industry   156

	Local Government	159
	Central Government and International	
	Government Agencies	161
	Other Institutions	162
Chapter 12.	**The Ownwork Agenda**	165
	Personal Incomes	165
	Access to Workspace, Land and Capital	173
	Local Economic Development	177
	Technology	180
	Education, Training, Leisure	182
	Economics, Social Sciences, Management	
	Sciences	183
	Key Institutions	184
Conclusion		189
Appendix 1	A Note on Paradigm Shifts	191
Appendix 2	An Ownwork Checklist	193
Notes and References		196
Publications Index		209
Name Index		213
Subject Index		217

Introduction

In Britain today several million people are unemployed. In the industrialised countries as a whole the number runs into tens of millions. For third world countries the situation is even worse. In 1982 the International Labour Organisation (ILO) estimated that a thousand million new jobs would have to be created by the year 2000 in order to achieve full employment worldwide. The Director-General of the ILO commented at the time: 'It has to be fully understood that there will be no situation of full employment if we are speaking of conventional employment.'[1] Things have got worse, not better, since then.

Most conventional politicians and economists still seem to claim, though with diminishing assurance, that their particular policies will bring back full employment in the long run. But, year by year, more and more people see these claims as utopian wishful thinking, if not downright deception. The impact of labour-saving technology, the competitive pressures of international trade, and the reluctance of taxpayers to finance more public service jobs, clearly suggest that, if substantial economic growth ever does come back as we still understand it, much of it is likely to be jobless growth. More and more people now feel in their bones, not only that many years of high unemployment lie ahead, but that full employment will never return again. They yearn for realistic and responsible leaders who will admit this possibility, and be prepared to respond to the new situation it implies.

The appropriate responses must be both practical and visionary. Practical action is needed urgently to ease the problems of the millions of people who face the prospect of unemployment now. Any society which continues to propagate the job ethic and to link basic incomes with jobs, but which leaves millions of people jobless, will continue to inflict great damage on those people and on itself. But, to be effective, practical action will also have to be visionary. The measures taken to alleviate the immediate problems of unemployment now will have to provide stepping-stones – and be seen to provide stepping-stones – to new ways of organising work, different from conventional employment, for the future.

As I shall show, there are three positive views about the future of work, leaving aside the purely pessimistic view that the present unemployment crisis will lead to disaster or continuing decline. The first is that something like full employment will return, and that employment will remain the normal and dominant way of organising work. The second is that full employment will not return, and that we have now begun the transition to a leisure society in which leisure will replace jobs as the central life activity for increasing numbers of people. The third is that full employment will not return, but that for increasing numbers of people it will be replaced by self-organised work, or 'ownwork'.

Ownwork means activity which is purposeful and important, and which people organise and control for themselves. It may be either paid or unpaid. It is done by people as individuals and as household members; it is done by groups of people working together; and it is done by people, who live in a particular locality, working locally to meet local needs. For the individual and the household, ownwork may mean self-employment, essential household and family activities, productive leisure activities such as do-it-yourself or growing some of one's own food, and participation in voluntary work. For groups of people, ownwork may mean working together as partners, perhaps in a community enterprise or a co-operative, or in a multitude of other activities with social, economic, environmental, scientific or other purposes in which they have a personal interest and to which they attach personal importance. For localities, the significance of ownwork is that it contributes to local self-reliance, an increased local capacity to meet local needs by local work, and a reduction of dependence on outside employers and suppliers.

The actual future will, of course, contain employment, leisure and ownwork – all three. There will almost certainly still be conventional jobs for many people; there will almost certainly be some increase in leisure, perhaps for most people; and ownwork will almost certainly play a larger part in many people's lives and in the life of society as a whole.

But it will be the third of these – the expansion of ownwork – that provides the key to the future of work and leisure. Only the expansion of ownwork will create conditions in which the problems of employment and leisure will be satisfactorily resolved. Only the expansion of ownwork will reflect the shift of values underlying the transition to a post-industrial future which has now begun. Only the expansion of ownwork can bring about the next stage in the liberation of work foreshadowed by the earlier historical progression from slavery to serfdom, and then from serfdom to employment.

That is the theme of this book. The book is directly concerned with the future of work in today's industrialised countries. But the same theme is powerfully relevant to the future of third world countries too. First, as ownwork plays an increasing part in the economies of the rich countries, those countries will become less exploitative of third world economies. Second, the principle of ownwork underlies the prospect of a new path of self-reliant economic development – 'another development'[2] – no less for the poor countries than for the rich. Third, in so far as people in the poor countries still look to the rich for the model of development to follow, the expansion of ownwork in the industrialised countries will support those in the third world who are trying to lead their countries along a more self-reliant path.

Part 1 of the book explores the three possible futures for work, and assesses how realistic each is. It reviews the key features of work during the employment age, and suggests that these will need to be fundamentally changed as part of the transition to a new work order for a post-industrial society. It gives a broad impression of what a shift of emphasis from employment to ownwork will imply, for example for energy, technology, the environment, leisure, education and training, money incomes, investment, and access to capital and land.

Part 2 examines how people's perceptions of work have changed in the past, especially in the transition from the middle ages to the modern period culminating in the industrial age. It discusses how the Protestant work ethic evolved, and what pointers this gives us now to the possible emergence of a new work ethic, based on ownwork, for the post-industrial age. It relates the rise of the Protestant work ethic to the change in worldview and values that marked the end of the middle ages and the beginning of the modern period; and it suggests that a comparable change in worldview and values is taking place today which will help to shape the new work ethic now. It considers the changes that have taken place in our ways of evaluating work, as an aspect of the development of economic theory, and suggests that further changes in economic thinking will accompany the shift from employment to ownwork.

Part 3 shows that the power structures of late industrial society have been shaped by the fact that employment has been the dominant form of work. It suggests, in particular, that today's organised labour movement, financial system, and system of representative politics and bureaucratic government can all be seen as superstructures arising out of the employment way of organising work; or, to put the same thing another way, that they are interlocking parts of an employment empire which has made the people of industrialised countries more and more dependent on it. The shift from employment to ownwork will erode the foundations of these superstructures, at least to some extent. In a sense, it will mark the end of the employment empire. In this end-of-empire process, many people now dependent on employment will face the challenge of liberating themselves from this dependence; and many people working within the existing power structures will be called on to decolonise them and to manage their decline constructively.

Part 4 fills out some of the detail of this approach. It deals with the practicalities of the shift to ownwork. It first shows that in many particulars this shift may already be under way and accelerating in the last few years. It then outlines an ownwork agenda, and examines how some of the changes proposed may be taken up by, and may affect, various sections of society – individual people, localities, businesses, government agencies and other professions and institutions. At the same time, Part 4 makes clear that no one should expect – or wait for – the ownwork agenda, and the shift from employment to ownwork, to be carried out according to any coherent or systematic plan. No government, for example, can realistically be expected to make the ownwork agenda a basis for its policy programme, until it has become clear to everyone that the shift towards ownwork is already far advanced. For the most part, the ownwork agenda will be carried out by the piecemeal interaction of initiatives and responses, the initiatives coming mainly from a wide diversity of individuals and unofficial groups, and the responses coming from the established institutions of society.

There is one further point to be made by way of introduction. I am sometimes asked what a society based on ownwork rather than on employment will be like and how it will function. Many detailed aspects of the answer to this question will be found in the chapters which follow. For example I see the move towards ownwork as a move towards a more self-reliant society, more decentralised, more equal as between men and women, better equipped with effective small-scale technologies, more committed to a high quality of life, and so on. But, in a more general sense, I believe the question itself is misleading. I have never thought it realistic to try to lay down a blueprint for a future society. For one thing, whatever may have happened in the past, I don't think a static society is likely to exist in the future. For another, I am more concerned with what is to be done now, than with the precise detail of what things may be like at some future date.

Rather than lay down a blueprint for an ownwork society, then, my purpose in this book is to convey a clear impression of the change of direction in the development of work that is needed now, as we step forward on the next stage of our journey from the past into the present and on into the future. We are coming to the end of the employment stage. We have reached the limit of progress in that direction. Two ways forward present themselves – the leisure route and the ownwork route. My aims are the comparatively limited, but practical, ones: of explaining why the ownwork route is the one we should take; of giving a reasonably clear idea of what is likely to be involved in setting out upon this new path now; and of providing material for discussion and further exploration towards that end (see Appendix 2 for a checklist of relevant questions).

In the last few years I have read many books, articles and papers about the future of work. I have taken part in numerous conferences and meetings on the subject, in North America, Australia, Scandinavia, and other parts of Europe, as well as in this country. These have been organised by businesses and business schools, government agencies, universities, professional organisations, religious bodies, and many different kinds of local groups. All over the industrialised world people are now asking what comes after full employment, and are beginning to confront the possibilities for change. I have learnt much from many of them.[3]

It would be impossible for me to acknowledge my debt to all who, in these and in other ways, have contributed to my thinking. Many are mentioned in the Notes and References at the end. Many others were mentioned in my last book.[4] But my main debt of gratitude, once again, is to my wife, Alison Pritchard. She has worked with me throughout. Her contribution has been indispensable.

PART 1

WHAT COMES AFTER THE EMPLOYMENT AGE?

In Part 1 we explore three possible futures for work, and assess how realistic each is. We review the key features of work during the employment age, and suggest that these will need to be fundamentally changed as part of the transition to a new work order for a post-industrial society. We give a broad impression of what a shift of emphasis from employment to ownwork will imply, for example for energy, technology, the environment, leisure, education and training, money incomes, investment, and access to capital and land.

Possible Futures For Work

A Post-Industrial Age?

At times of uncertainty like the present, different people perceive the future in different ways. There are at least three distinct views about the future of work. The keyword for the first is employment. The keyword for the second is leisure. The keyword for the third is ownwork. They are based on three distinct perceptions of the future of industrialised society. I call these Business As Usual, HE (Hyper-Expansionist) and SHE(Sane, Humane, Ecological). Business As Usual assumes that the society of the future will not be very different from late industrial society as it is today. HE and SHE are contrasting visions of a post-industrial society which, in either case, will be distinctly different from the society we have today.

Some people dislike the term 'post-industrial'. They find it an ugly, woolly word that tells us nothing about the future. They say it is no more informative than if we called the great transformation of the 18th and 19th centuries the 'post-agricultural' revolution, and the age which it brought in the post-agricultural age. And they point out that industry will continue to exist for the foreseeable future.

However, the idea of a post-industrial future does suggest that we are coming to the end of the period of history which we call the industrial age, and that a new age is beginning. It helps to prepare us for the possibility of a post-industrial transformation of society no less fundamental than the industrial revolution brought in. It prompts such questions as: what will post-industrial society be like? And what do we want it to be like?

As a matter of historical fact, the term 'industrial revolution' did not come into use until long after the main events to which it refers, by which time the defining characteristic of post-agricultural society had become clear. We do not yet know

what the most apt description of the post-industrial age will
be. Those who now try to describe it as the Space Age, or the
Age of Aquarius, or the Communication Age, or the Information Age, or the Age of Automation, or whatever, are
usually doing no more than emphasising the aspect of the
post-industrial era which particularly interests them.

So far as industry is concerned, of course it will not cease to
exist in the post-industrial age, any more than farms and
churches ceased to exist when the industrial age came in. The
point is that, just as the dominant features of industrial society
were quite different from those of the agricultural and
religious society which it succeeded, so the dominant values,
lifestyles, practices, institutions and modes of thought in a
post-industrial society will be different from those that have
been dominant in the industrial age.

Two Visions of Post-Industrial Society[1]
One vision of post-industrial society – the 'HE' vision of the
future – might more accurately be described as superindus-
trial. It is a vision of a future based on big science, big technology and expert know-how. Its dominant drives and
features would be those of industrial society accentuated and
writ large. One of its most prominent exponents, the futurist
Herman Kahn, used to say that we are now only half way
through the period of expansion and growth that has been
typical of the industrial age. We have had 200 years of it, and
there is another 200 years to go.

By contrast, the 'SHE' vision of the future foresees, not an
acceleration along the same path of development we have
followed during the industrial age, but a change in the direction of development. According to this view, the industrial
revolution marked a huge advance in the capacity of human
beings to control and harness the material world. It vastly
extended the technical limits to human achievement, and
amplified our physical capabilities – to travel, to communi-
cate, to build, to provide ourselves with heat and power and
light, to produce all manner of goods and commodities, and
to organise ourselves in millions for peace and war. Today it
has brought about changes in the institutions of society and in
people's personal lives that few people living 200 years ago
could possibly have foreseen, or even imagined. So, as the

industrial age comes to an end, a comparable transformation may be in prospect – a post-industrial revolution which could bring about an advance no less far-reaching than the industrial revolution did. This time, however, the breakthrough will be primarily psychological and social, not technical and economic. It will enlarge the human limits to human achievement. It will amplify our capacity to develop ourselves as human beings, together with the communities and the societies in which we live. Not only will it bring fundamental social and personal change, as the industrial revolution did, but that is what will be its main motive force.

These two contrasting visions of post-industrial society have emerged quite clearly in the last few years. Some of their main values and tendencies are shown in these two columns.

HE	SHE
quantitative values and goals	qualitative values and goals
economic growth	human development
organisational values and goals	personal and inter-personal values and goals
money values	real needs and aspirations
contractual relationships	mutual exchange relationships
intellectual, rational, detached	intuitive, experiential, empathetic
masculine priorities	feminine priorities
specialisation/helplessness	all-round competence
technocracy/dependency	self-reliance
centralising	local
urban	country-wide
European	planetary
anthropocentric	ecological

These two visions of a post-industrial future provide the two poles, and the two clusters of ideas and possibilities, around which serious discussion of the future, including the future of work, is likely to revolve from now on. The following pages outline some of the practical differences between them and 'Business As Usual'

Three Futures For Work
The Business-As-Usual view of the future of work is still

Three Possible Futures

Work

Full employment can be restored, and employment will remain the dominant form of work. Other activities (e.g. housework, family care, voluntary work) will continue to have lower status. Sharp distinctions will continue to exist between education for the young, work for adults, and retirement for the old; and between work and leisure.

HE
Full employment will not be restored. All necessary work will be done by a skilled elite of professionals and experts, backed by automation, other capital-intensive technology, and specialist know-how. Others will not work. They will merely consume the goods and services provided by the working minority – including leisure, information and education services. Society will be split between workers and drones.

SHE
Full employment will not be restored. Work will be redefined to include many forms of useful and valued activity in addition to paid employment. Paid and unpaid work will be shared around more equally, e.g. between men and women. Part-time employment will be common. Many different patterns of working will be possible, according to people's circumstances and preferences. Households and neighbourhoods will become recognised workplaces and centres of production. Young and old will have valued work roles. Work and leisure activities will overlap.

Money Incomes	Paid work will continue to be the primary source. Society will continue to provide a basic income to people who fall outside this norm, but such people, if of 'working age', will continue to be stigmatised as exceptions.	The skilled working elite will be highly paid. Proponents of this scenario have not yet worked out through what channels everyone else will receive an income. From dividends, after nationalisation of all production? Or from benefits financed by high taxation? Or as wages from menial jobs?	Society will pay everyone a basic income as of right, enabling them to choose how they will divide their time between paid and unpaid activities. People who do not need this extra income because they earn more on top of it will have it taxed back automatically.
Technology	New technologies will continue to be developed for their own sake, because scientists and design engineers find them challenging, and because industries and governments hope they will prove profitable and that people can be persuaded to use them. There will also continue to be opposition to many new technologies on the grounds that they may be dangerous, exploitative, wasteful, polluting and socially undesirable or unnecessary.	Even more effort and resources than at present will be channelled into the development of new technologies. It will be accepted that all problems have technical solutions, and that top priority should always be given to the technical approach, including the development of new forms of expertise and reliance on the decisions and advice of experts. Opposition to this approach will become weaker. Technology will be master.	The development and diffusion of certain types of new technologies and new skills will have high priority. These will be technologies and skills which enhance the capacities of people to do more for themselves and one another, and reduce their dependence on outside systems, organisations and professional expertise. In particular, small-scale (including micro-processor) technologies will greatly expand people's capacities to work for themselves and one another in their own homes and localities. This scenario is not anti-technology. Technology will have an important role, but as servant.

Economy

BUSINESS AS USUAL

Economic growth can be restored. Creation of wealth by industry and commercial services can continue to support publicly financed social services. Industrialised economies will remain centralised, and big business and publicly owned corporations will retain their dominant role. Formal economic activity will continue to be the only kind of economic activity that really matters, and informal economic activity will remain unimportant.

HE

Economic growth will only be achieved by concentrating on high technology production and by marketing highly professionalised services. The wealth thereby created will meet society's needs. Formal economic activity will become even more dominant. Multinational business will have an even more dominant role.

SHE

The most important areas for economic growth and social progress will be in the informal economy. People's energies will be released to create wealth and welfare for themselves and one another in their own households, neighbourhoods and localities. The fact of so many people finding satisfactory occupation in this way will remove many existing obstacles to the efficient functioning of the formal economy. Within the formal economy, local small-scale enterprise will be the main growth sector. Localities will become more self-sufficient economically and less dependent on outside employers and suppliers.

Planning and Housing	Urban industrialised patterns of lifestyle, employment and movement will continue to be the norm. Residential and work locations will remain in separate zones. Planning regulations will continue to assume that people use their homes for leisure and consumption activities only. Houses will continue to be designed that way. The land, premises and equipment that people need for their work will continue to be provided by employers.	The coming of the leisure society and the information age will help to reshape the built environment. People will have more leisure time to spend at home, at local leisure facilities (swimming pools, sports centres, etc.), and on trips away from home. The provision of new leisure facilities (including education) will make big new demands on space. What precisely this will mean, for example in old inner city areas, is not yet clear.	As more of people's work, leisure, learning and caring activities centre on their homes, neighbourhoods and localities, new demands for space and facilities will arise there. Today's house designs, zoning arrangements and planning regulations will become inappropriate. More people will participate in planning and building their own houses and environment. There will be more shared, multi-family households and clusters of houses, including housing cooperatives. More people will need land, premises and equipment for their own work. Residential densities will fall, in the old city centres as elsewhere, and the tendency will be toward more dispersed patterns of settlement country-wide.
Transport	Traffic and transport patterns will continue much as they are today.	A decline in travel between homes and places of work will be matched by a rise in travel for leisure.	A decline in travel between homes and places of work will only be partly matched by a rise in travel for leisure.

	BUSINESS AS USUAL	HE	SHE
Energy	Patterns of energy use and energy development will continue much as at present. Changes will mainly be prompted by adjustment to price changes and the balance of supply and demand.	Demand for energy will continue to grow. Dependence on capital-intensive, centralised, high technology sources of energy (e.g. nuclear power) will grow. A few centres of energy production will supply the whole populace of energy consumers. A 'hard' energy path will be followed.[2]	Less energy-intensive patterns of working, living and transport, coupled with conservation and more efficient ways of using energy, will reduce demand for energy. Energy production will be more decentralised. There will be a tendency to greater energy self-sufficiency in regions and localities – and even, to some extent, in households where energy conservation, heat pumps, solar panels, etc., will reduce the need for energy brought in from outside. A 'soft' energy path will be followed.[2]
Food	Patterns of food production, processing, distribution and consumption will continue to be dominated by agribusiness farming, industrial manufacturing, and the distribution of processed and packaged foods through supermarket chains to standardised consumers.	As for Business As Usual, but with more emphasis on new agricultural and nutrition technology. For example, more productive strains of animals and crops will be developed; beneficial elements (e.g. vitamins) will be added and harmful ones (e.g. fats) will be removed as a normal aspect of	There will be, as for energy, a tendency to greater food self-sufficiency. More people will grow food, either as small farmers, part-time farmers and smallholders, or (for themselves) in their own gardens and allotments. Food production will be more decentralised and food distribution chains will

be shorter. Food cooperatives will become more numerous. Home cooking will be the norm. Multi-family purchasing and feeding arrangements may become more common.

food-manufacturing and processing. People will eat out more often; fast-food chains will be part of a food service industry expanding in response to the growing 'leisure market'.

Education and Learning

As at present, education will take place in educational institutions at the hands of professional educators. It will continue to be primarily for young people, before they enter the age bracket in which they will be expected to have a full-time job. Its main aims will be to provide them with the credentials to get and hold down a job, and to socialise them into what will remain a mass-employment, mass-consumption society. Main criteria of a good education will continue to be the certificates and diplomas that one can show for it, and the jobs which it opens up.

Education will divide into two main branches. The first will qualify a person for a high status job as a member of the technocratic and professional elite. The second branch will teach people how to use their leisure. Its status will be somewhat lower. Both types of education will, in principle, be lifelong. In the high technology, leisure society of the information age, education will be one of the biggest growth industries. Openings for professionally qualified, expert educators will greatly expand.

Education will be for capability. It will help people to learn life-skills of all kinds – physical, intellectual, inter-personal, emotional. It will be geared to a pattern of living in which most people expect to have part-time employment and also to undertake a good deal of useful, rewarding activity for themselves and their family and neighbours. It will recognise that people often learn better from doing things with experienced people than from receiving class-room instruction from professional educators.

Health

BUSINESS AS USUAL

Individuals and society will continue to give lower priority to the promotion of health than to the treatment of sickness. 'Health services' will continue to be primarily sickness services, and people's perception of themselves as consumers of those services will continue to dominate their perception of health. The main debate will continue to be whether sickness services should be provided commercially or at public expense.

HE

Medical technology will solve most health problems. Genetic screening, organ transplants, new drugs, computer monitoring and computer records will eliminate or control congenital diseases and handicaps, enable the body to be maintained in good operating order, and enable expert physicians to deal more quickly and effectively than today with their patients' problems – a widening range of which, such as bereavements, losses and failures, will become subject to medical treatment. Health promotion and sickness prevention may increase somewhat. But the increased dominance of medical experts and technologists will ensure that today's remedial bias remains strong.

SHE

Greater personal responsibility for health will lead people to the positive cultivation of their health and to the positive promotion of a healthy physical and social environment. Higher priority will be given to nutrition, public health and the psychosomatic aspects of health than is given today. Personal self-help and cooperative mutual aid in matters of health and sickness will be more highly rated than dependence on the expertise of health professionals. People will learn to manage the health hazards and stressful transitions in their lives. Nurture and care will be emphasised, in contrast to the 'heroic' interventionism of the HE future.

| **Principles** | Mass employment, mass consumption. Dependence on institutions for work and for goods and services. Obligation to be employed. Organisational values, masculine values, anthropocentric values. Interventionist, instrumental mode of action. Analytical, reductionist mode of thought. | Mass leisure, mass consumption. Continued dependence on institutions. Increased dependence on technology and experts. A schizophrenic society: the working elite will be hard-working, responsible, and highly motivated; the masses will enjoy leisured irresponsibility. Technocratic values dominant, including even greater emphasis on organisational, masculine, anthropocentric values, etc. | A shift towards self-help and decentralisation in production of goods and provision of services. Reintegration of people's work with other aspects of their lives. This will bring new meaning to life. Personal values, feminine values, ecological values. Experiential mode of action. Intuitive mode of awareness. |

voiced, though with diminishing conviction, by politicians and economists of all mainstream persuasions, and by most business leaders and trade union leaders, in all the industrial countries. They do not question, at least not in public, that employment will remain the dominant form of work and that full employment ought to be restored. They suggest that it can be restored if the particular policies which they support are adopted. For some this means bringing back high levels of employment in conventional manufacturing industry. For others it means replacing jobs lost in manufacturing by a great increase of jobs elsewhere: in information services like computing and telecommunications; in sectors of the knowledge industry like research and consultancy; in social services like education and health; and in leisure industries and services like sports, entertainment, and travel. Some hope that, by making the economy internationally competitive, the resulting creation of wealth will automatically generate enough jobs for all. Micawberlike, they ask us to have faith that new jobs will turn up, though they cannot tell us what these jobs will be or how they will be created. Others, by contrast, hope that by insulating the national economy from international competition and by planning it centrally, they will be able to organise enough jobs for all.

Because we have become so accustomed to these various expressions of the Business-As-Usual view, we have tended to forget how much they take for granted and, until quite recently, we have often failed to notice how large an element of utopian wishful thinking they contain.

The HE view of the future of work appeals to many scientists, technologists, industrialists and business commentators who, as most people do, see the future primarily from their own point of view. They expect the existing polarisation between skilled and unskilled workers, employed and unemployed, to continue to the point where all the important work is done by a minority of highly skilled and highly responsible people. These people will be putting the space colonies into orbit, installing and monitoring the automated factories, managing the nuclear power stations, running the psychiatric institutes and genetic laboratories, operating the communications networks, and carrying out all the other highly skilled tasks on which a super-industrial society will depend. The rest of us will be living lives of leisure. As in past societies, the prevailing pattern of work in the HE future will reflect a division between superior and inferior members of society. But the division will no longer be between masters and slaves, lords and serfs, employers and employees. This time it will be between workers and drones. The working minority will monopolise all the important work and exclude the rest of the population from it – at best permitting them to undertake marginal, menial tasks.

Because we have become accustomed to accept the authority, in their own specialist fields, of those who support the HE view of the future of work, we have sometimes tended to forget the political, social and psychological realities which it ignores, and have failed to notice how large an element of utopian, 'mad scientist' fantasy it contains.

The SHE view of the future of work, by contrast, sees the historical progression from masters-and-slaves to lords-and-serfs and then to employers-and-employees as an unfinished progress towards greater equality. It now envisages a further step in that direction. As hopes of restoring full employment fade away, the dominant form of work will no longer be seen as employment but as self-organised activity. In other words, many more people will take control of their own work. They will work on their own account, to meet their own needs, to achieve their own purposes, in their own households and local communities, on a personal and inter-personal basis, to a very much greater extent than the prevailing pattern of work in the industrial age has allowed them to do. The direction in which work will develop in the SHE future will represent a reversal of some of the dominant trends of the industrial age. Thus, as we shall see, the informal economy* will become one of the main areas for further economic growth and social progress. A fulfilling, well-balanced life will be regarded as one that offers a flexible choice of work patterns; and part-time work in the formal economy and part-time work in the informal economy

---

* In principle, I use the term 'informal economy' to include activities in which people do things for themselves and one another without being paid, as contrasted with the 'formal economy' in which work takes the form of paid employment. In practice, the distinction is often blurred. For a fuller discussion, see Chapter 7.

will come to be seen as the norm. Ownwork will be the characteristic form of work in the new work order.

Because the majority of people in late industrial societies
have perceived themselves as dependent employees and consumers, and because powerful interest groups of all kinds
have done everything they could to reinforce that perception
of social reality, it has been easy to dismiss as a romantic, utopian dream the idea of a new work order based on ownwork. It
is only in the last few years that this idea has begun to be realistically appraised, as a practical response to the worsening
prospects for conventional employment.[3]

A Realistic Assessment

If we ask which of our three futures – Business As Usual, HE and SHE – the actual future of work is most likely to resemble, the realistic answer must be that it is almost certain to contain elements of all three. To some extent, work will continue to be organised as jobs and money incomes continue to be linked with employment. To some extent there will continue to be a widening gap between the activities of the more highly skilled members of society and their less highly skilled fellow citizens, a general increase in leisure, and a weakening of the link between employment and income. And to some extent there will be a revival of local economies, a growth of self-organised work, and a blurring of work and leisure. A realistic approach to the future of work and the problems of unemployment must therefore encompass all three views of the future. Public policies should do so, business strategies should do so, and so should people's plans and thoughts about their own working lives.

However, if we ask which of the three visions opens up the most helpful new insights from a practical point of view, we find that a great deal of weight must be given to the prospect of ownwork and the SHE future.

The Four-Sector Economy
One useful way of looking at it is to divide the economy into four sectors, and to consider the future prospects for work in each.[1] The first sector contains big industry – the capital-intensive, highly mechanised activities of extraction and production such as mining, oil, chemicals, heavy engineering, steel, ship-building, motor-manufacturing, and so on. The second sector contains big services – the hitherto more labour-intensive commercial service activities like banking and insurance, and public services like education, health and

welfare. The third sector contains small local enterprises, including conventional, small profit-making businesses, but also including a growing range of community businesses, community associations, residents' associations, local voluntary activities, amenity projects and other new kinds of local enterprise. The fourth sector is the household and neighbourhood sector, consisting of conventional forms of home-based paid work including self-employment, and conventional forms of unpaid work like housework, but also including a growing range of activities that provide goods and services directly for oneself, one's family and one's neighbours, such as food growing, home improvement, the servicing and repair of vehicles and equipment, and many forms of self-provided entertainment and care.

There is general agreement that, in the big industrial sector, job losses will almost certainly continue to outweigh the creation of new jobs. This sector has to compete internationally, and its costs must be competitive with those in other countries – not only the mature industrial countries of Western Europe and North America, but also the newly industrialised nations, especially of the Far East, whose labour costs are still comparatively low. This will mean using the most efficient and advanced technologies, including automation and the microprocessor. And that will mean shedding more jobs. In fact, the big industrial sector is in a Catch-22 situation, so far as the future of jobs is concerned. Either these industries will be modernised successfully enough for them to be internationally competitive, which will involve reducing jobs. Or they will not be modernised successfully, they will become uncompetitive, and they will then have to be further slimmed down with the loss of many jobs. Either way, the realistic assumption must be that the big industrial sector will offer fewer jobs in the future than it does today.

In the big services sector, the last two decades have seen more jobs being created in banking, insurance and other financial and commercial services. But this is unlikely to last. Office automation will lead to substantial reductions in staff. Restructuring in the financial services industry, such as is now taking place in the City of London where the old demarcation lines between building societies, banks, the stock exchange, and so on are breaking down, may have a similar effect. If there should be a financial collapse, or an end to the long-term expansion of financial institutions and the long-term growth in the role played by money in our lives (see Chapter 9), this too would reduce the number of jobs in financial and commercial services.

The question is whether these prospective job losses in financial and commercial services will be offset or even, as has been claimed, more than offset by new jobs in information and communication industries like computers and cable television, in leisure industries, and in public services like education, health and welfare.

Tom Stonier[2] is one of those who argue that 'the major problem confronting western governments in the 1980s is the need to devise ways of effecting a smooth transition from an industrial to an information economy – to shift labour from the manufacturing to the knowledge industries. In part the answer has to involve a massive expansion of an updated education system to provide new, mainly information skills which will be useful in a post-industrial economy'. Stonier will not be surprised if 'the education industry becomes the number one employer over the next few decades'.

However, it is almost certainly naive to assume that in 30 years' time millions more of us than today will be employed in the kinds of jobs that produce information and education. There will be a limit to the amount of information that people will be prepared to buy. And, as we have seen in the last ten years in all the industrialised countries, including countries like France and Sweden and Britain and Germany that have had socialist or social democratic governments, the prospect of financing a massive expansion of employment in services like education and health is very slim. Some people say it would be possible to find the money for a huge expansion of jobs in these services if the will to do so existed. But this misses the underlying reality. This is that employment is now becoming an uneconomic way to organise many kinds of work. The nature of the employment relationship is now making it increasingly difficult to get work done by employees on terms, and to a standard of performance, which are acceptable both to them and to the other parties concerned. We shall return to this point later in this chapter.

At all events, it is little more than wishful thinking to suppose that enough new jobs will be created in the big services sector to offset job losses elsewhere in the economy. It would be very unwise to assume that full employment will eventually be restored that way. It is more realistic to expect a declining, or at best a stationary, level of jobs in the large-scale services sector.

This leaves us with the local enterprise sector and the household and neighbourhood sector. The declining number of jobs in the two big sectors of the economy, big industry and big services, means that more people will be spending more time in the local and household sectors. The amount of work done in these two sectors will certainly expand. But, although some of this will be in the form of conventional jobs, much of the new work will not take the form of regular, conventional employment, but rather it will be casual, and much of it either unpaid or semi-voluntary.

As we shall see, the prospect of a very substantial expansion of useful activity in localities, neighbourhoods and households is of central importance. Not only does it provide the key to a hopeful, indeed a better, future for work, it also offers hope for dealing with many of the other economic and social problems that late industrial societies now face. But before going further into that aspect we should thoroughly satisfy ourselves that a great increase in ownwork is, in fact, unavoidable; and that no acceptable outcome from the present unemployment crisis will be achieved merely by creating new jobs, or by expanding leisure, or by some mixture of the two.

Restoring Full Employment – A Realistic Goal?
Apart from the hope that jobs lost in the industrial sector will be replaced by new jobs created in the services and information sector, the arguments put forward by those who still say they think employment will remain the normal form of work and that jobs can be made available for all who want them, are broadly of three kinds. They rely on the possibility of economic recovery in the short term; on the possibility of economic recovery in the long term; or on a continuing reduction in the time worked by employees.

The possibility of recovery in the short term can be quickly disposed of. Few people now seriously believe that short-term economic recovery could restore full employment. Politicians may continue to claim that employment will pick up as the recession comes to an end, and that their particular policies will help to make this happen. But many people now understand that, if significant economic growth does take place in the next three or four years, much of it will be jobless. There are not many who see a realistic alternative to continuing high unemployment for some years to come.[3]

The possibility that full employment might eventually be restored by a new burst of economic growth in the longer term is based on the theory of long waves, or 'Kondratieff cycles', named after the Russian economist who worked them out and who died in one of Stalin's Siberian camps in the 1930s.[4] Kondratieff showed that, since the industrial age began, there has been a recurring pattern of economic prosperity and decline. The first long wave began to rise in the 1780s, peaked around 1810 and sank back into deep depression by about 1840. Beginning from that point the second long wave rose to its peak in the 1860s and fell back to its trough in the 1890s. The third long wave peaked about 1920 and fell back into the deep depression of the early and middle 1930s. A fourth long wave peaked around 1970. It can be expected to continue falling until it hits bottom some time in the early 1990s. At that point, assuming the long-wave cycles continue to repeat, the fifth long wave will start to rise. We might expect to get back to full employment some time around the year 2000.

The Kondratieff cycles of the industrial age have been associated with marked bursts of technological innovation. For example, the huge explosion of railway building in Britain after 1840 coincided with the upswing of the second long wave; the rise of the internal combustion engine and electricity were associated with the third; and so on. The theory is that the introduction of new technologies triggers the new long wave; then, as the wave proceeds, effort shifts to diffusing those technologies more and more widely through the economy, and for a time further technological invention and innovation slows down. In due course the time comes when the diffusion of that wave of new technologies can go no further; the downswing then begins. Eventually, the whole process starts again with a new burst of technological innovation.

The argument, then, is that if we wait for another 15 years

and if the fifth Kondratieff cycle proceeds according to expectation, we may eventually get back to something like full employment. We have the prospect of 15 more difficult years immediately ahead, but, so the argument goes, that is no reason for casting aside the assumption that full employment will eventually be restored and that employment will continue to be the dominant form of work.

But think again about this. Can we wait another 15 years? Shall we be able to leave it, as in the past, to the cycle of technological innovation and change eventually to restore the conditions for full employment? May not social forces compel us to legitimate new ways of organising work and new ways of providing people with their money incomes, before another 15 years of high unemployment have passed? Unless, long before that time, some way is found of relieving the damaging effects of unemployment on people's income, social status and personal self-respect, the society of the late 1980s and 1990s is unlikely to be prepared to endure continuing high unemployment as peaceably as did the society that existed in the previous downwaves of 50, 90, 140 and 200 years ago.

And what if the industrial age is coming to an end? We cannot necessarily assume that the long-wave pattern of prosperity and slump, together with its effects on employment, that has prevailed during the industrial age will prove a reliable guide for the post-industrial future. As I have suggested, we may well have now reached a stage of economic and social development in which employment is becoming an increasingly difficult way to organise many kinds of work on terms acceptable to all the parties concerned. These include principally employees, employers, customers and (where public services are concerned) taxpayers. The increasing difficulty of organising work in the form of employment has presented itself most clearly as disagreements about pay and money: employees are only willing to work for rising levels of pay which employers, customers and taxpayers feel they can less and less afford. (Attempts to dodge these disagreements have been a principal cause of inflation in recent decades.) These financial difficulties are reinforced by features of employment that are absent from other forms of work – the way employers and employees feel about each other, and the management procedures, trade union practices, and government interventions that go with the employment way of organising work.

As I have said, the fact is that employment now seems to be becoming an uneconomic way of getting work done. (The same thing happened to slavery in its time, as both Adam Smith and Karl Marx understood very well.[5]) This being so, employers will continue, as a general rule, to try to reduce the number of their employees, and many potential employers will continue to try to avoid employing people altogether. Employers and potential employers alike will from now on aim to minimise their dependence on employment, and to find other ways of getting work done. At the same time, as job opportunities continue to become more scarce for people who would still choose to be employed if they could, more and more of them will decide to seek other ways of working. This new factor may very well override the link between economic upswing and returning full employment which has characterised the cyclical long waves of the industrial age.

The third main argument used to support the idea that employment will continue to be the dominant form of work, and that employment will eventually become available for all who want it, is that working time will continue to fall. People in jobs will work fewer hours in the day, fewer days in the week, fewer weeks in the year, and fewer years in a lifetime, than they do now. This will mean that more jobs will be available for more people. This, it is said, is the way we should set about restoring full employment.

There is no doubt that something of this kind will happen. The shorter working week, longer holidays, earlier retirement, more sabbaticals, job-sharing – these and other ways of reducing the amount of time people spend on their jobs – are certainly likely to spread. A mix of part-time paid work and part-time unpaid work is likely to become a much more common work pattern than today, and a flexilife pattern of work – involving paid employment at certain stages of life, but not at others – will become widespread. But it is surely unrealistic to assume that this will make it possible either to restore full employment, or to maintain employment as the dominant form of work.

In the first place, so long as employment remains the overwhelmingly important form of work and source of income for most people that it is today, it is very difficult to see how reductions in employees' working time can take place on a scale sufficiently large and at a pace sufficiently fast to make it possible to share out the available paid employment to everyone who wants it. Such negotiations as there have recently been, for example in Britain and Germany, about the possibility of introducing a 35-hour working week, have highlighted some of the difficulties. But, secondly, if changes of this kind were to take place at a pace and on a scale sufficient to make it possible to share employment among all who wanted it, the resulting situation – in which most people would not be working in their jobs for more than two or three short days a week – could hardly continue to be one in which employment was still regarded as the only truly valid form of work. There would be so many people spending so much of their time on other activities, including other forms of useful work, that the primacy of employment would be bound to be called into question, at least to some extent.

To sum up, the prospect of a successful return to conventional full employment, whether through short-term economic recovery, or through a long-term economic upswing in some years' time, or through a reduction in the time worked by employees, does not provide any more realistic a basis for dealing with the present crisis of unemployment and work, than does the simple assumption that jobs lost in industry will be automatically replaced by new jobs in services. Common sense and compassion now demand that we work out the implications of this – in other words, that we examine the possibility of encouraging other activities in place of employment, of enabling people to receive an income in other ways than from employment, and of removing the causes of personal distress and social damage that now attach to the condition of being unemployed.

Leisure In Place of Work – A Realistic Goal?
The idea that in a post-employment society employment could be largely replaced by leisure activities, and that increasing numbers of people could live lives of leisure, is open to serious question from two points of view.

First, many people without employment would resist the idea that they were expected to make no useful contribution, either towards meeting their own needs or towards meeting those of other people, and were merely expected to keep themselves amused and out of trouble. They would resent the sense of uselessness and futility which this would imply, and feel that their lives were condemned to be empty of value and meaning. It is not as if most of us today are heirs to an aristocratic tradition of cultured leisure. We have inherited the protestant work ethic, and the need to feel useful which goes with it.

Second, many of the people still in employment would resent the idea that they were expected to support large numbers of idle drones. The situation would be one in which the employed were perceived as doing all the useful work and the unemployed were seen, on a larger scale and a more permanent basis than today, as making no useful contribution to society. People's feelings would be very different from what they would be if being employed were seen as only one of a number of ways of doing useful work and of making a positive contribution to society.

The question of how to finance the leisure of the unemployed in a leisure society would thus be a difficult one. They would need a money income. Thus some extension of today's unemployment and social security benefits systems would be needed, perhaps going as far as the introduction of a Guaranteed Basic Income (GBI).(See Chapters 4 and 12 for further discussion.) But this would be much more difficult to introduce in the context of a society clearly split between workers and non-workers, than in the context of a society in which it was understood that the purpose of the basic income was to give all citizens the freedom to choose their own mix of paid and unpaid work.

Finally, if anything resembling the leisure society did come about, one thing is sure. Many of those at leisure would in fact use their time for useful activities of many kinds. In other words, they would find ways of working on their own account, to provide useful goods and services for themselves and for one another. A leisure society would automatically transform itself, at least to some extent, into an ownwork society.

In short, the prospect of moving towards a leisure society cannot be accepted as providing any more realistic a solution to the present crisis of unemployment and work, than the hope of an eventual return to full employment. A vital element is missing. This is the expansion of ownwork – that is, work undertaken, often in forms other than conventional employment, in the local and household sectors.

The Significance of Ownwork

The actual future of work, as I have said, will be one in which employment, leisure and ownwork will all have a part to play. One aim must be to improve the existing organisation of employment – from several points of view, including greater efficiency of results, more satisfying conditions of work, and fairer distribution of the jobs which are available. Another aim must be to provide improved opportunities for leisure. But no less important than either of these will be to make possible a great expansion of ownwork – in fact, there are compelling reasons for giving this priority over both employment and leisure.

The first is that the expansion of ownwork will be a necessary precondition to achieving the other two aims. Indeed, a significant expansion is probably the only means now of creating conditions in which an internationally competitive economy and a firmly founded welfare state can flourish. This is because the development of productive and useful work in the local and household sectors will reduce the present dependency of localities and households on jobs provided by the large-scale manufacturing and service sectors of the economy, as well as on goods and services purchased from these sectors or provided by them at public expense. This reduction of dependency will have a double significance. In the first place it will contribute directly to the wellbeing of the localities and households concerned, many of whom are today suffering unemployment and hardship as a result of failed dependency on employing and social welfare organisations outside their own control. But also, by relieving the big manufacturing and services sectors of their present function of providing routine work and routine services for localities and households which could organise such work and provide such services for themselves, the expansion of ownwork will free those organisations to become more efficient in their own proper spheres. This will help big firms to become more competitive in international markets, and enable the big service organisations like the National Health Service to concentrate on the provision of sophisticated, specialist services, like hi-tech hospital facilities, which self-help and mutual aid at local and household levels clearly cannot provide. In other words, the revival of the household and local economies, and the expansion of the kinds of work that contribute to them, will be a vital precondition for the successful further development of the big organisations of the national economy and the welfare state. It will, in fact, be the essential feature of any successful strategy to improve the efficiency and the international competitiveness of the economy as a whole.

Another important reason for giving priority to an expansion of ownwork is that it represents a new departure, a positive change of direction, from the industrial-age path of development that we have been on for the last 200 or 300 years. If we concentrate on employment or leisure as the nub of the problem, we stay stuck in the assumptions and categories of thinking of the industrial age. Exploring how to encourage ownwork enables us to identify many obstacles to further progress that arise directly from those old assumptions.

A preliminary exploration of that kind is in Chapter 4. But first, in Chapter 3, we shall look at some of the main characteristics of employment that have evolved during the industrial age. This historical background illuminates, by contrast, a number of features of work that will be important from now on.

The Age of Employment

Employment has been the way that industrial societies and the industrial age have organised work. In no other societies and in no other period of history has work been organised that way.

Pre-Industrial Patterns of Work[1]
In pre-industrial times most men and women worked in and around their homes. The household was a place of production and work. Its work was linked into the work of the local village community. People provided the necessities of life for themselves and their families. Money, therefore, played a smaller part in their lives than it does in ours. Most of their work was unpaid.

Men and women divided the household tasks between them. Children helped their parents at work as soon as they were old enough; they got most of their education that way. The older generation helped, too; grandmothers looked after the younger children at home, while their parents were out working in the fields. Work, like other activities, was thus an integral part of family and local life. Not only were many of today's particular specialisms unknown, but more generally, the economic and social spheres of work were not then distinguished as separate domains. The creation of wealth and the provision of welfare were not treated as separate functions. The production of goods and the provision of services by people for themselves and one another were interwoven threads in the fabric of daily life.

It would be wrong to romanticise the nature of the family and village life and work in pre-industrial times. Very few people in today's industrial societies would want to return to that way of life. Most people then were poorer and less healthy than we are today. Their lives were shorter and less secure.

They had virtually none of the technology that we now have, and little knowledge of science or of the wider world beyond their own locality. They had few of the entertainments, holidays and travel opportunities open to us today. For many there was no escape from the tyranny of the local squire; and, for many women and young people, there was no choice but to accept their subordinate position in the patriarchal household.

Nonetheless, the prevailing pattern of work had convivial[2] features which employment today often lacks. Self-service, self-help, self-reliance and co-operative mutual aid were characteristics of that way of life and work. Economic and social relationships then were predominantly personal and interpersonal, not impersonal and organisational as they are today. People generally had ready access to the means of production – the land, buildings, equipment and livestock they needed for their work. No one then foresaw the day when people would be dependent on employers to provide them with the wherewithal for work, and when people would have no work to do unless employers were able and willing to organise it for them.

The Situation Now

In late industrial society the situation is quite different. Men and women alike have been taught to look outside the home for work – for the kind of work that brings in money. We need far more money than our pre-industrial ancestors did, to pay for the goods and services that we no longer provide for ourselves and one another. Moreover, we have become dependent on paid work and other work outside the home to give us a sense of identity, a social role, that the diminished functions of our households and immediate neighbourhoods can no longer supply. Most of us need such work to enable us to meet people, and to provide us with a way of structuring our time – needs which the isolated, unproductive homes of late industrial society have become less and less able to meet. 'I'm only a housewife' sums up the sense of deprivation, loss of personal confidence, and lack of social status experienced by the typical contemporary homeworker.

This change in the pattern of people's lives has been one of the most important features of the way society has developed during the industrial age. Once that direction of development had been established, it was cumulative and self-reinforcing. As more and more people looked to paid work outside the home, so they became less and less able to meet the needs of those – especially the young and the old and the sick members of their families – who had previously depended on their presence at home. So, increasingly, those dependents had to look outside the home too, to institutions like schools and hospitals, for their education and care. And that, in turn, created new jobs in those institutions – new openings for paid employment – which pulled more people away from work in their homes.

Employment as Dependency

This change in the dominant pattern of work has transformed people's lives and the life of society. The effect on people's freedom to control their own work has been one of its most important features.

Before the industrial age all human societies, except perhaps hunter-gatherer tribes, had been societies of superiors and inferiors. In ancient societies slaves had worked for their masters, and in medieval societies serfs and villeins had worked for their lords. Such societies had not claimed to be societies of free and equal, fully developed people, in command of their own work and sharing its fruits with their fellows. Now that employees worked for employers, did this represent progress?

In theory, the replacement of serfdom and villeinage by paid employment should have been a step forward. Relieved of their old feudal obligations to their lords, people on the face of it became free to offer their work as equals in the market place to anyone who would buy it. In the last 200 to 300 years many self-made men made out successfully in this way,[3] and for many women over the years the opportunity of employment outside the home came as a liberation.[4] But for many people the change from feudal to industrial-age patterns of work had the opposite effect. More powerfully than ever before it compelled the majority of the population to work for other people. It resulted in the division of society into two nations – employers and employees – as society had never been divided before.[5] As Christopher Hill puts it, 'What most men felt was not that new doors had been thrown open but that old rights had been taken away.'[6]

In England, the pressure started in the 16th century when the monasteries were dissolved. With the resulting break-up of the great feudal estates, most of the villeins were turned into landless wage-labourers. Later the enclosures of the 17th and 18th centuries deprived the common people of their rights to graze cattle, pick up timber, and hunt animals on the common lands, and further increased their dependence on paid labour. This was well understood at the time. Enclosure of the commons was positively praised by contemporaries in the knowledge that it forced labourers to 'work every day in the year', and that 'their children will be put out to labour early'.[7] By depriving them of any chance of economic independence, the 'subordination of the lower ranks of society would be thereby considerably secured'. Harsh penalties had been imposed on the workless poor under the Poor Law from the the 16th century, and harsh restrictions on labour mobility under laws such as the great Statute of Artificers of 1563. Enclosures now made doubly sure that for people who had no property there was no escape from a semi-servile state and from their 'duty to work for their betters'. So a pool of ready labour became available for employers.

The coming of the factory system drove work out of the home and brought a further loss of independence at work:

Weaving had offered an employment to the whole family: the young children winding bobbins, older children watching for faults, picking over the cloth, or helping to throw the shuttle in the broad-loom; adolescents working a second or third loom; the wife taking a turn at weaving in and among her domestic employments. The family was together, and however poor meals were, at least they could sit down at chosen times. A whole pattern of family and community life had grown up around the loom-shops; work did not prevent conversation or singing. The spinning-mills – which offered employment only for their children – and then the power-loom sheds which generally employed only the wives or adolescents –were resisted until poverty broke down all defences.[8]

Masculine, Impersonal Work

Another feature of the employment age was the split that developed between men's work and women's work. As employment became the dominant form of work in the 19th and 20th centuries, the father typically became the bread-winner going out to work, the mother the housewife staying at home. Money loomed large in people's lives, with the paid work of men enjoying a higher status than the unpaid work of women. Eventually this led women to insist that they should have rights to employment equal with those of men, and women now have a somewhat fairer deal where paid work is concerned. But progress towards equality has been lop-sided; most men still remain unwilling and unable to do their fair share of the unpaid work of running the household and rais-ing the family. They continue to assume that the really import-ant work is that done for employers for pay, and so they give it priority. Most men have lost sight of the possibility that they might devote their energies to their own purposes, and work directly for the wellbeing and development of themselves, their families, their neighbours and their friends.

As industrialisation progressed, the impersonal character of employment, and of industrial society as a whole, became more marked. In its early stages the employer/employee relationship often remained a personal one, as it does in many small businesses today. Employer and employee perceived each other as individual people, and dealt with one another that way – humanely or brutally as the case might be.[9] But the technologies typical of the industrial age required division of labour and specialisation of work. They thus favoured large-scale organisation. Having pulled work out of the home into the factory, the new industrial technologies then led to the replacement of small factories by big ones. Partly for this reason – and partly because both capitalism and collectivism treated workers as subordinate instruments of larger imper-sonal purposes – personal control of employees by employers came to be replaced by impersonal management systems.

At the same time, the urbanisation of work brought with it a less personal, more anonymous, way of life in the great indus-trial cities and towns. Moreover, as rail and then road transport became established, people commuted longer and longer distances to work. In today's late industrial society, many people have come to accept that the energies which they channel into their work will be expended far away from their nearest and dearest, and on purposes unconnected with their home and the locality in which they live.

So, although most people have come to take for granted the form of work, i.e. employment, which has been dominant in the late industrial age, many have experienced it as disconnected from other aspects of their lives and as having comparatively little intrinsic value of its own. Many, perhaps most, employees have not expected to achieve a serious purpose of their own or a meaning for themselves through their work. They have worked in order to be paid and in order to achieve self-esteem, social respect, companionship and time-structure to their daily life. Typical in this respect of their age and social background were a group of young people studied in the Manchester area during the 1970s.

For those youngsters work is something to be endured in order to acquire the resources to enable the further enjoyment of non-work activities. It has no intrinsic value and nothing to commend it as an inherently worthwhile activity – though, of course, certain sources of satisfaction can be found and these enclaves are highly prized as the primary source of day-to-day diversion: 'Good mates', 'getting around', 'having a laugh'. Nevertheless it is not an area in which they locate any potential for personal achievement or improvement, and their interests and more meaningful activities are either peripheral to, or entirely divorced from, it.[10]

Job dissatisfaction has always been widespread among adult workers too. For example, 'For the many there is a hardly concealed discontent. The blue-collar blues is no more bitterly sung than the white-collar moan.'[11] And: 'We find the blues of blue-collar workers linked to their job dissatisfactions as in the disgruntlement of white-collar workers and the growing discontent among managers. Many workers at all occupational levels feel locked in, their mobility blocked, the opportunity to grow lacking in their jobs, challenge missing from their task.'[12]

Exclusive Nature of Employment

However, the only alternative to a job which has been open to most people in late industrial society – unemployment – cannot provide the self-esteem, social respect, companionship and time structure that people seek from work. People who have not had employment, or have been ineligible for it, have been made to feel inferior. Women are not the only members of society whose work status has been downgraded during the industrial age by the ever growing dominance of employment over other forms of work. People reaching retirement age have been made to feel their useful life is over. Teenagers not yet eligible to join the labour market have been made to feel they can make no useful contribution. Unemployed people of working age have been made to feel excluded and marginalised. Law and custom have dissuaded old, young and unemployed alike from doing useful work of an informal kind. Unemployed people have even been forbidden to commit themselves to voluntary work or to self-chosen courses of education and training, on pain of losing their unemployment pay. The choice has tended to become a simple either/or – *either* you have a job, *or* you don't work; *either* your contribution to the economy takes the form of a job, *or* you are perceived as a burden and a cost to be carried by those who do have jobs.

These general pressures pushing everyone eligible into employment have been reinforced by many others of a more specific kind. Until very recently, personnel managements have discouraged part-time jobs, especially for men. Pension practices have discouraged flexible working lives and early retirement. Social security arrangements have encouraged single parents to seek full-time employment. Trade union pressures have sought to reserve work for full-time employees. As continually inflating land prices have made it more difficult for ordinary people to buy land, and as the numbers of small firms and small farms have declined over the years, the opportunities for self-employment have declined, too. Only in the last year or two have there been signs of change.

In short, so far as individual people are concerned, the continually growing dominance of employment as a way of organising work has tended to limit people's freedom to work for their own chosen purposes and in their own chosen ways. It has tended to limit their satisfaction in work if they are employed, and to exclude them from what is regarded as useful work if they are not. It has kept them dependent on increasingly remote employers to provide them with work, and has made them vulnerable to decisions about their work which are right outside their own control.

Dependency of Local Communities
Much the same has happened to the work of localities as has happened to the work of individual people during the employment age. Local work has become increasingly controlled by decisions taken elsewhere. Just as households lost control over their own work, so towns and districts lost control of theirs. Just as people became enmeshed in the impersonal forces of the labour market, so local communities became enmeshed in the impersonal forces of national and international economies. Just as the work of people became vulnerable to events far removed from their own lives, so the work of local communities became vulnerable to economic cycles, industrial innovations, and other events far removed from theirs. Throughout the industrial age, increasing specialisation and division of labour locally, regionally and nationally diminished the capacity of local communities to organise their work and secure a livelihood for themselves, just as personal specialisation and division of labour diminished that same capacity in individual people.

At the pre-industrial stage of development most local communities, like most households, were much more self-sufficient than they are today. Work done locally met a greater proportion of local needs – for example, for food, clothing, shelter, heat and power. External trading, accompanied by the earning and spending of money outside the local community, was a smaller part of economic life in most places than it is today.

As the industrial age progressed, local control of the economic aspects of life seeped away. Just as most people became dependent on employers to provide them with work, so – similarly – most localities became dependent for their work on employing organisations based elsewhere. Just as most people ceased to be able to provide themselves with the necessities of life and became dependent on buying them in, so – similarly – most localities became dependent on goods and services brought in from industries and public service organisations based elsewhere. Just as most people became dependent on earning in and spending out money, so – similarly – many local communities came to be dependent on money coming in from outside and going straight out again, not circulating locally and thereby supporting local work. Just as in late industrial society the family and the household came to be perceived as part of the social rather than the economic domain, so the sphere of local government came to be perceived as primarily social, not economic. It is only in the last few years that in Britain, for example, local authorities have begun to take on responsibilities for local employment and local economic development.

An extreme example of local economic dependency can be found in some tourist districts. It is most obvious in islands – as, for example, in Greece. In the tourist season, as the boatloads and planeloads of tourists come in, they are accompanied by boatloads and planeloads of food for them to eat, liquor for them to drink, souvenirs and other holiday goods for them to buy, and people to serve them in the restaurants and hotels. Little self-sustaining local production or work is generated. When the season is over, the tourists go home. All they leave behind is rubbish – and the local people waiting for the next tourist season.

That is, as I say, an extreme example. More typical forms of economic dependency and vulnerability, found all over the industrialised world, are where local economies have become dependent on industries like ship-building, steel-making, railway repair and manufacture, automobiles, nickel-mining, coal-mining, or whatever other industry it may be, controlled by national or multinational companies, or by national governments or international government agencies, based outside the district. As the economic climate has changed and these industries have gone into decline, two things have become apparent. First, the people who take decisions about the future of these industries have no particular commitment to the localities affected; they live elsewhere themselves; they are absentee landlords of their industrial estates – absentee worklords, you might say. Second, the people in the affected localities, having specialised in those industries and having become dependent on them, have lost whatever alternative skills and resources and alternative traditions of work they might once have had. They now have no capacity to organise work for themselves, which they can fall back on. They are in a very vulnerable position.

In response to this situation, in many parts of the industrialised world in recent years, representatives of central governments and local authorities have been competing with one another to attract new national and multinational employers to their cities and districts. They are all looking for new industries which will replace the old steel, or shipbuilding, or other, industries whose decline has left high unemployment. In thus seeking to replace the old absentee worklords with new ones, development agencies everywhere have blindly sought to perpetuate the vulnerability of local communities to employment decisions outside their own control. So deeply rooted is the assumption that work must be externally provided, that it has hardly occurred to these agencies to consider the possibility of helping their communities to build up greater local economic autonomy, including the capacity to organise local work to meet an increasing proportion of local needs.

In the third world, too, the growing dependency of local economies on outside control has followed much the same principle. They became dependent on the cultivation of cash crops for export to the industrialised countries. All over the third world local people were persuaded, and often compelled, to grow export crops like coffee, tea, tobacco, cocoa, cotton, sisal, rubber and sugar, instead of using their land and developing their skills to grow food, timber and other crops for their own use. Markets for these cash crops have been altogether outside local control, and terms of trade have usually been unfavourable. Moreover, the production of these crops has typically been controlled by companies based outside the country concerned – absentee worklords again. Work which is organised and controlled in this way is bound to be dangerously vulnerable to decisions and developments over which the workers themselves have no control at all.

As labour costs have grown in the industrialised world in recent years, multinational companies have begun to move their manufacturing operations to the third world, adding the features of local economic dependency that have been characteristic of the industrialised world to those that have accompanied the production of commodities and cash crops for international markets. In recent years multinational companies have also been stepping up their efforts to make third world people more dependent on the purchase of consumer products, babyfoods being probably the most notorious example. One consequence, as of any extension of the consumer society, has been to deepen people's dependence on paid employment to provide them with money to spend on consumer products which they cannot provide by their own efforts for themselves.

Limits to Employment

To sum up, two key features of the path of development that has characterised all industrialised and industrialising societies have been: the increasing dominance of employment over other forms of work; and the increasing subordination of local work and local economies to outside control. The principle in both cases is the same. Just as individual people in their own households have lost the freedom, and the capacity, and the habit, to meet their own needs directly by their own work, and have become more and more dependent on paid employment outside their own control to provide them with money to buy goods and services, so local communities have lost the freedom, and the capacity, and the habit, to meet their needs directly by their own work. They too have become more and more dependent on externally organised work to provide an inflow of money from outside, which is then spent on buying in from outside the goods and services required to meet local needs.

In short, as the industrial-age way of organising work as employment has become ever more deeply engrained in the structures of industrialised and industrialising societies, it has turned work into a form of activity which is dependent, remotely controlled, and instrumental. Work in the post-industrial age will have to develop in a positively different direction. It will have to become more autonomous, more self-controlled, and more directly related to the needs and purposes of those who are doing the work. As we reach the end of the employment age, it is becoming urgent to think out how to reverse some of the main features of employment as a way of organising work.

4

A Change of Direction

The change of direction to new, post-industrial patterns of work will affect every aspect of human life and society just as profoundly as they have been affected by the rise of employment during the industrial age. This chapter gives a broad impression of some aspects of this, and identifies some of the industrial-age assumptions that will have to be reversed. The practicalities of the transition to ownwork will be considered in greater detail in Part 4.

As the last chapter made clear, the nature of work in the industrial age has meant that the work of people and communities has tended to be exploited for purposes not directly connected with their own needs, or their own purposes and values. This impersonal aspect of industrial-age work, and the lack of a sense of personal and local responsibility for the results of work that it has brought with it, have also contributed to another important feature of work in the industrial age – its concentration on the exploitation, consumption and destruction of natural resources. The vision of a SHE future, with ownwork as a characteristic feature of it, foresees a new work order that is: *saner*, in the sense that people and communities will have greater control over their work and greater opportunities to use it directly to meet their own needs, including the need for healthy self-development; more *humane*, in the sense that people's work will not only be less exploited for purposes alien to them, but will also be less exploitative and damaging to other people; and also more *ecological*, in the sense that work will be more concerned with ways to live harmoniously and sustainably with the natural environment, than with ways of exploiting it. These basic features of work in the post-industrial age will have many practical implications.

Energy

Work is closely related to energy. The word 'work' is derived from the Greek word for work, *ergon,* and the word 'energy', also derived from the Greek, refers to that which has work in it. In other words, energy is the capacity for work. In science an 'erg' is a unit of work or energy.

Throughout history the kinds of work people have done and the ways they have worked have been connected with their uses of energy. People have used the energies of other human beings; of creatures like horses, cattle, donkeys and elephants; and of the sun, wind and water. They have also used energies derived from such vegetable and fossil fuels as wood, oil, coal and gas.

The industrial age has been the fossil-fuel age. Its prime source of energy has been first coal, then oil. The availability of these fuels, and the prevailing techniques for obtaining and using them, have affected the very nature of work. So one question we must ask is: What will *post*-industrial society use as its energy base? And what will this mean for work?

The HE vision of post-industrial society assumes that nuclear power will steadily replace existing, unrenewable sources of energy. Such a society would thus be centralised. In its provision of energy, it would be a Big Brother society, split between an expert minority of producers – a technocratic elite – and a dependent majority of consumers – the latter denied the opportunity of playing any part at all in meeting either their energy or their other basic needs.

The change of direction we envisage, however, in accordance with the SHE vision of post-industrial society in which ownwork is the norm, is towards a society more *de*centralised and self-reliant in its provision and use of energy, and in all else. Efficient use and conservation of energy will reduce its consumption, and therefore its need; the development of renewable energy sources like the sun and wind will remove the need to develop nuclear power; and the harnessing of such sources at local and household levels will mean that many more people, not fewer, will play a part in meeting their own and others' energy and other basic needs.[1]

Moving in this new direction will also enable many more people to channel their psychic, as well as their physical, energies into useful work. An important characteristic of the post-industrial age will be a freer flow of people's energies into the central activities of their lives.[2]

Technology
It was not only in meeting people's needs for energy – for warmth and power and light – that the technologies of the industrial age drove work out of households and local communities into factories and offices, cities and towns. They have had that effect on every kind of work. Thereby, they have been socially divisive. The cottager can afford a handloom, but only the factory owner can afford a powerloom. The smallholder can afford a plough, but only the agribusinessman can afford the agricultural technologies of the 1980s. Only the richer Indian peasant can afford the technologies of the 'green revolution', which then transform his poorer neighbours into his hired labour.

The Business-As-Usual view of the future assumes that technology will still have this social effect on the organisation of work. People will typically continue to work as employees for employers, because only employers will be able to afford large-scale technologies and have the capacity to manage large organisations. The HE vision expects advances in technology to accentuate the split in society between the elite workers and the drones. The big technologies of the super-industrial future – nuclear power stations, automated chemical plants, automated production lines, factories in space, and so on – would be controlled and operated by a very small number of people. The rest of us would become redundant as workers. As consumers we would become even more dependent than we are today on big technologies and organisations, and on the people who operate them and manage them.

The change of direction towards ownwork, on the other hand, will reflect the fact that miniaturisation is now the new frontier of technology. Whereas the technology of the industrial age drove work out of the home and the neighbourhood, and deprived most people of the freedom to control their work, the technology of the post-industrial age will make it possible to reverse this trend. Already the washing machine has largely replaced laundries, and the home computer and many other advanced small-scale equipments and 'user-friendly' materials for building, decorating, repairing, servicing,

heating, plumbing, electrics, food growing, food preparation, clothing and furnishing, are coming in. In a few years'
time small, programmable industrial robots will be available,
costing little more than the present price of a family car. This
will make it possible for small engineering workshops,
attached – like garages – to people's homes, to provide local
markets with many kinds of goods which economies of scale
have reserved for mass production during the industrial age.
The technology of the SHE future will be the technology of self-
service, self-employment and self-reliance – the technology of
a society which enables free people to choose their own
work.[3]

Environment
The dominant pattern of work in the industrial age, and the
ways in which we have used energy and technology, have
significantly affected the environment in which we live.

First, there have been changes that we tend now to take for
granted. The houses and the cities, towns and villages we live
in have been shaped, and have shaped themselves, around the
dominant work culture, i.e. employment. We now live in
houses which, for the most part, have been designed as places
of consumption and leisure rather than as places of production and work. Domestic architecture on the one hand and
industrial and commercial architecture on the other have
evolved to serve two separated functions and to meet two
separated sets of needs. Similarly, in our cities, towns and
villages the areas where people live are generally separate
from the areas where they work. Planners have been taught
that people work on employers' premises, and have learned to
separate the spaces needed for living and working into distinct
residential and industrial zones. Planning regulations positively prevent many people from working in or around their
own homes today.

Patterns of transport, similarly, reflect the dominant pattern
of work. A sizeable proportion of rail and road traffic is com-
muter traffic, that is people travelling from their homes to
their places of work in the morning, and back again at the end
of their working day. Much of the rest is business traffic –
transport of goods and materials, and travel by people in the
course of their work. This reflects today's high degree of divi-

sion of labour and specialisation of work. People in their own place cannot now provide themselves with the products, services and skills they need. These have to be transported in from elsewhere.

Then there have been the changes to the environment that we notice as destructive and damaging. New ways of working in agriculture have damaged the countryside, for example by farmers grubbing up hedgerows and woodlands.[4] New industries have polluted water and air with chemicals. Heavy lorries travelling through residential communities have spoiled people's quality of life. New roads, new housing, new airports, new factories have spread a blanket of concrete over more and more land. Globally, today's ways of working are destroying the rain forests, polluting the atmosphere and the rivers and lakes and oceans, altering the climatic balance, and eliminating growing numbers of living species. Increasing numbers of people are beginning to question ways of working and living that put at risk the biosphere, the fabric of life, of which we ourselves are part.[5]

The Business-As-Usual view of the future, which assumes that employment will remain the dominant form of work, takes for granted that today's patterns of housing, planning and transport will remain basically unchanged. Insofar as the Business-As-Usual view admits that further 'progress' of a conventional kind may have damaging environmental effects, it relies on conventional methods of restriction and control – legislation, financial inducements, international negotiation – to limit the damage so caused.

Since the setback to the credibility of tower blocks and other aspects of the technocratic approach to housing and planning that was typical of the 1960s and early 1970s, proponents of the HE vision of the future have said little about the housing, planning and transport implications of a leisure society in which most people would have no work. Their assumption seems to be that, as people became even more dependent as consumers and clients on organisations and professionals than they are today – fast-food chains, cable television, universities for the elderly, bereavement clinics, and so on – new technologies and new forms of professional expertise would enable housing, planning and transport to adapt as necessary. So far as damage to the environment is concerned, the HE view appears to take it for granted likewise that scientific and professional expertise and the development of new and improved technologies will provide the necessary solutions.

The change of direction which we envisage, however, will be based, at least partly, on recognition that the prevailing patterns of housing, planning and transport are closely linked to the damage now being done to the environment. Both stem from the kind of work that has been dominant during the industrial age – work which has exploited people and nature alike as if both were expendable resources. The patterns of housing, planning and transport, and of industry and agriculture, towards which a saner, more humane, more ecological future will require us to move, will be those reflecting the new assumption that ownwork is the normal form of work. And such a society will by its very nature be more conserving of the natural environment.

In practice, this change of direction means that we must begin to plan and build *now*.[6] For example, more space will be required in and around people's homes for productive work. When new neighbourhoods and localities are planned and developed, provision should be made for space and facilities that will enable local production, e.g. of food and energy, to make a contribution to local consumption. These will be particularly important features of *urban* redevelopment, where the existing physical structure of the old inner cities reflects the centralised, mass-production, mass-consumption, employment-dependent character of the declining industrial-age society.

Leisure[7]

As employment became the dominant form of work, the distinction between work and leisure became sharper. The word 'leisure' means free time, and leisure activities came to mean what people did in the time they had to themselves, as contrasted with work which was what people did in the time claimed by their employer. This distinction between work and leisure has always been clearer for employees than for people who have organised their own work, like housewives or the self-employed. This is linked with the fact that, in general, men in industrial societies have tended to enjoy more leisure than women.

Another distinction between work and leisure became sharper as employment became the dominant form of work. As work increasingly came to be activity which brought in money, so leisure increasingly came to be activity on which money had to be spent. A widening range of leisure industries and services grew up providing leisure goods and leisure facilities. Some of these were in the so-called private sector; people purchased leisure goods like hi-fis and services like package holidays from them directly. Others were in the so-called public sector; these were paid for out of public expenditure, financed by taxation, and the goods and services which they provided – like public swimming pools – were available to people free or at a reduced cost.

The shift from informal to formally organised work during the industrial age was thus paralleled by a comparable shift in the sphere of leisure. Whereas in pre-industrial societies most people organised leisure, like work, for themselves and one another, in late industrial societies they became dependent on the organisations of the formal economy to provide them with leisure activities as well as providing them with work.

One way of thinking about the future of leisure, as about the future of work, is to ask who controls people's time.

Employment has meant that employees lose control of their working time by selling it to their employers, and employers gain control of their employees' time by buying it from them. Something similar is true of leisure. As leisure industries and services have developed, people at leisure have increasingly spent their time on activities devised for them by others, including commercial organisations and public services. By contrast, in self-organised leisure – as in ownwork – people take control of the use of their own time. (There is, incidentally, a close connection between control over time and control over space. Employers normally control their employees' workspace, just as they control their worktime. Most employees have no workspace of their own. Similarly, leisure-providers normally control the space, as well as the time, used for leisure by their customers and clients.)

As people are required to spend less time in employment, they will have more time for leisure. The HE vision of post-industrial society foresees people spending most of this extra free time consuming leisure products and in leisure activities provided by leisure industries, leisure services and organised entertainment. People's leisure will be mainly outer-directed, just as their work has been outer-directed in employment. The SHE vision, on the other hand, foresees people using their increased free time in accordance with their own perceptions of value and need. The use they make of it will blur the distinction between leisure and ownwork.

Another way of thinking about the future of leisure is to distinguish between leisure activities that have to be paid for and leisure activities that do not – just as one way of thinking about the future of work is to distinguish between work that people get paid for and work that they do not. For example, there are leisure activities and facilities which cost a substantial amount of money. Foreign holidays are one example. Local authority sports centres are another. There are also leisure activities which cost comparatively little money, like walking or reading. Thirdly, there are leisure activities which save money. If you grow your own food and do your own repairs, you can eat better and live better for less money. Fourthly, there are leisure activities which can be turned into money-earning activities. Hobbies like photography and keeping chickens might be examples.

The Business-As-Usual view of the future of work assumes that leisure industries and services will continue to grow. The assumption is that people will still have jobs, and so will still have money to purchase leisure goods and services and to pay taxes and rates for public leisure facilities. The growth in this category of leisure is itself expected to be a source of new jobs.

The HE view assumes that many people will not have jobs, and will be dependent on being provided with leisure activities to fill their time. In this case, there would be a sharp distinction between the leisure-providers, who would be skilled and dedicated workers, and the consumers of leisure, who would play little part in providing or organising leisure for themselves – just as, more generally, most people would play little part in meeting any of their own needs. The question of how these leisure activities would be financed, when many of the people enjoying them would not be earning incomes from employment, is one to which we shall return.

As already outlined, a change of direction towards ownwork

and the SHE future will involve a shift of emphasis away from leisure industries and services to leisure organised by people for themselves. The dividing line between ownwork and this kind of leisure will often be difficult to draw. People will make use of their leisure – the increasing amount of time at their own disposal – to do useful work on their own account, on their own interests and on their own projects. Leisure activities will then shade into a much wider range of work and activity options than most people have today, when for most people leisure is what they have when not at work, and the two main options are either to work or to be unemployed.

Education and Training
Education and training in industrial society have been geared to the assumption that work means employment. For most people the purpose of education has been to prepare them to do a job; the better their education, the better the job they have been likely to get. Similarly, most training has been aimed at preparing the trainee to function better as an employee in a particular job. At the same time, a comparatively small elite have been educated, not to become employees, but to take their place as members of the employer class. One of the key social divisions in education during the industrial age has thus been related to the social division between employers and employees. That social division was typical of industrial society at its peak. It has retained its cultural and social significance in late industrial society, even though many supposedly superior people – such as top company executives, heads of universities, and internationally renowned scientists – are employees of the organisations in which they work.

The Business-As-Usual criticism of education in recent years is that education has failed to prepare people properly for employment. The outstanding new initiatives in Britain, for example, have been to do with Youth Training and Work Experience, in the sense of giving young people education, training and experience that will equip them to be more effective as employees.

The HE view of the future, on the other hand, stresses the need for education in two particular fields. For potential members of the technocratic elite, education should concen-

trate on instilling the skills needed for using and developing
the new advanced technologies, for example in the micro-
electronic and bio-engineering fields. For the mass of the
people, by contrast, the key should be education for leisure,
and education should concentrate on preparing them to use
the leisure time that will loom so largely in their lives.

A change of direction towards ownwork will involve a shift
of emphasis towards education and training in the practical
skills, including the personal and interpersonal skills, that will
help people to live rewarding lives outside employment, to
make productive use of their leisure, and to do useful and
satisfying work of their own. Education for resourcefulness,
self-sufficiency, and co-operative self-reliance will be what is
most needed.

Incomes

People who live in late industrial societies have to have a
money income in order to buy the goods and services
required to meet their needs. As a rule, we are able to meet few
of our own needs directly by our own efforts, as our pre-
industrial ancestors largely did.

Late industrial societies accept an obligation to ensure that
all their citizens do receive a money income sufficient to enable them to subsist. But the assumption still is that the normal way to get this income is from paid employment, either
directly as an employee or indirectly as a dependent of an
employee. People who get their income from the state, for example, in the form of unemployment benefit or social security
benefit, are treated as unfortunate exceptions to this general
rule. They are regarded as second-class citizens, and are subjected to severe restrictions. These limit their freedom to commit themselves to useful activities, such as training or voluntary work (since these might make them unavailable to take a
conventional job, if one existed), and heavily discourage them
from trying to build up paid work on their own account.

The Business-as-Usual view thus assumes that people who
don't have a job can do no useful work; that, if they want to
work, they should look for a job; and that the main objectives
of government policy should be to encourage this, while creating conditions in which enough jobs will once again be available for all.

Both the HE and SHE views of the future believe that these assumptions are out of date. They both believe that the high level of unemployment which is in prospect for the next 10 or 15 years will mark a transition to a new work order in which full employment will have become a thing of the past. They both foresee that it will then no longer be normal for most people to receive their money income in the form of wages or salary from a job, and that it will have to become regarded as normal for people to receive their money income in other ways, including regular payments from the state. They both believe that this must lead to an extension of the present system of personal benefits, and its consolidation with the personal tax system, in the form of an unconditional subsistence income or Guaranteed Basic Income (GBI). All citizens would then receive an adequate untaxed basic income from the state, and (in most versions of the idea) be allowed the freedom to top this up with additional taxed income if they chose to do so.

The HE vision of a leisure society looks upon the GBI as providing a basis on which most people would be able to live lives of leisure. But, as I suggested in Chapter 2, this raises questions to which no answers are yet in sight. The level of income required by people who were expected to do no useful work of their own and to make no useful contribution to meeting their own needs and other people's would have to be quite high, and remain so permanently. The resulting financial problems and the resentment of those who were still doing paid work and paying taxes on their earnings to support the leisured, might make this a difficult arrangement to sustain.

The SHE vision on the other hand, sees the most important function of the GBI as a transitional one. It will facilitate the change of direction to a new work order in which many people will be enabled to do more work on their own account and meet a greater proportion of their own needs by their own efforts. They will then, in aggregate, become less dependent than people are today both on the benefits system to provide all their income if they are unemployed, and on other arms of the present welfare state to provide them with social services. In other words, the GBI will enable many individual people who are now unemployed or otherwise caught in the poverty trap which the present system of benefits imposes, to make the transition to the point where they can earn a taxable income on their own account; and, by freeing people from the need to work in useless jobs or to spend their time searching for non-existent jobs, the GBI will give them more time to care for themselves, and one another. By thus reducing people's dependence on benefits and welfare services, the GBI will help to reduce the cost of the welfare state and the level of taxation needed to support it. It may even be possible to hope that, as over the years people generally become rather more able to do things for themselves and rather less dependent than they are today on money to buy what they cannot provide for themselves, the level of GBI required by most people to support a decent life could eventually fall. (The GBI scheme is further discussed in Chapter 12.)

Capital, Investment, Land
During the industrial age the assumption took root that employers would provide the land, the premises, the equipment and other forms of capital assets and working capital needed to support people's work.

The Business-As-Usual view of the future takes for granted that this will continue to be the case. Investment grants and other forms of financial assistance, as well as depreciation allowances to be set against tax, should therefore continue to be given to employing organisations to encourage them to invest in creating and maintaining jobs. Because employment is assumed to be the only valid form of work, it follows that employers should continue to be given this special treatment, even though it amounts to discrimination against investment in other types of work, for example in the household or local community. The HE view, while not agreeing that the creation of employment will or should continue to be a function of productive investment, accepts nevertheless that large enterprises will and should continue to be the main owners and controllers of productive capital assets, that the most important forms of production will still be those which are large and heavily capitalised, and that today's system of financial institutions channelling flows of investment from people to organisations will continue to provide a valid pattern for the future.

The SHE view, on the other hand, foresees a change of direction in this respect as in others. The shift from employment to ownwork will involve a shift in the ownership and control of productive capital assets from employing organisations to people themselves. In particular, new mechanisms and new institutions will be needed to enable people to channel their savings into investment in small-scale local activities of their own choice, including local employment initiatives of co-operative, socially beneficial types which will improve the locality in which the investor lives. New ways will have to be introduced to enable people with little or no capital of their own to build up 'sweat equity' for themselves, for example by helping to build their own houses and to develop their own new communities. New forms of land tenure, including land-holding by community land trusts and community develop-ment trusts, may be needed to enable people without capital to build up a shared stake in the land which they need for their work. More generally, new ways will have to be found for decentralising the ownership and control of land, and making it available to people and local enterprises needing land for their work, on terms which they will be able to afford. Part 4 contains further discussion of the practicalities.

PART 2

CHANGING PERCEPTIONS OF WORK

In Part 2 we examine how people's perceptions of work have changed in the past, especially in the transition from the middle ages to the modern period culminating in the industrial age. Against that historical background we consider how people's perceptions of work may be expected to change again in the post-industrial transition.

Chapter 5 discusses how the Protestant work ethic evolved, and what pointers this gives us to the emergence of a new work ethic for the post-industrial age. Chapter 6 relates the change in perceptions of work to the change in worldview and in values that took place as the middle ages came to an end. It suggests that a comparable change in worldview and values is occurring now which will help to shape the new post-industrial work ethic. Chapter 7 discusses the changes that have taken place since the middle ages in our ways of evaluating work as part of the development of economic theory and practice. It suggests that a further change of this kind will be one aspect of the transition from employment to ownwork.

5

The Work Ethic Evolves

From time to time in history an old worldview is replaced by a new one. A change comes over the way people perceive themselves, other people, their society, the natural world around them, and the supernatural or the divine. Thus the dominant perceptions and attitudes of the industrial age have been different from those of pre-industrial times, and those of post-industrial society are likely to be different again. These shifts of perception, shifts from one worldview to another, that mark the transition from one age to another, correspond to what are now known as paradigm shifts in science. (See Appendix 1 for note on latter.)

Ever since the hunting and gathering way of life gave place to settled agriculture – that is, since Adam and Eve were driven out of the Garden of Eden – work has played a central part in the lives of most human beings. Our experiences and perceptions of work are shaped by, and help to shape, all our other experiences and perceptions. They are of a piece with our experiences and perceptions of ourselves, other people, society, nature, and supernature. So if the industrial-age paradigm of work as employment is to be replaced by a post-industrial paradigm of work as ownwork, this is likely to be part of a larger change of worldview associated with the transition to a post-industrial age.

In this chapter and the following two we shall explore a number of ways in which people's outlook changed between the middle ages and the industrial age, and may be expected to change again now. We shall look at the links between these changes and people's perceptions of work and their attitudes towards it. The rise of the Protestant work ethic is a good point at which to start.

The Protestant Reformation

At the heart of the Protestant Reformation was a shift in people's perception of reality. Medieval society had been predominantly religious; people then perceived this life as a preparation for the life hereafter; they perceived the life hereafter, and the duties and activities centring around it, as more real and more important than the worldly duties and tasks pertaining only to our life here on earth. The shift began when Luther, rebelling against the sterility and corruption of the Catholic Church of his time, preached that the monastic life had little value as a means of justifying oneself to God, and that monastic renunciation of the duties of this world was a selfish withdrawal from more important obligations, Luther argued that the fulfilment of worldly duties was the way to live acceptably to God; that these duties stemmed from obligations imposed upon the individual by his position in the world; that to fulfil them was his calling; and that every legitimate calling had worth in the eyes of God.

In thus shifting the emphasis to worldly work, Luther was helping to reshape people's perceptions of what was real. A similar shift is under way today. People are beginning to perceive that real life and real work are lived and done by persons, in touch with themselves, with one another, and with the natural world and universe around them; they are beginning to be aware that real life is not, after all, to be found in the organisational world of business, government, and finance. These, like the church hierarchies of the late middle ages, are becoming increasingly remote; they have to call on increasingly elaborate structures of theoretical argument – now economic, then ecclesiastic – to bolster their legitimacy; and they are becoming increasingly bogged down in problems of their own making. Just as Luther taught people to see the Catholic Church as a buffer between themselves and reality, so we are beginning to see the organisational structures of the formal economy as buffers between ourselves and reality today.

Calvin took the Lutheran rethink a stage further. He preached predestination: some people – the elect – were predestined to be saved; the rest were predestined to be damned. The psychological effect of this doctrine was what Max Weber called 'the unprecedented inner loneliness of the single individual', following an anxious path towards a destiny decreed from eternity. This new experience of individualism and spiritual isolation brought a less personal attitude to the fulfilment of daily tasks and social obligations, and a sense that 'labour in the service of impersonal social usefulness' was what promoted the glory of God. To stave off their anxiety, people needed proof that they were among the elect. So the 'self-confident saints whom we can rediscover in the hard Puritan merchants of the heroic age of capitalism' committed themselves to intense worldly activity to disperse religious doubt and bring the certainty of grace.[1]

Initially, then, Calvinism embraced worldly work not because it was thought to be a *means* of attaining salvation, but rather because it was seen as a *sign* of salvation to come. It was seen as the technical means, not of purchasing salvation, but of avoiding the fear of damnation. However, this distinction was easily blurred. In the course of time many Protestants came to believe that God helps those who help themselves. They came to assume that work could actually contribute to their salvation, not just give them confidence that they were already saved. So the idea of self-help began to modify the earlier Lutheran concept of a calling.

Luther had kept to the traditional medieval view that each person should remain in the calling in which God had placed him, and that people should confine their activities within the limits imposed by their station in life. Luther had taken for granted what Tawney calls 'the traditional stratification of rural society. It is a natural, rather than a money economy, consisting of the petty dealings of peasants and craftsmen in the small market town, where industry is carried on for the subsistence of the household, and the consumption of wealth follows hard on the production of it, and where commerce and finance are occasional incidents rather than the forces which keep the whole system in motion'. Calvinism, on the other hand, was largely an urban movement. Based originally in Geneva and gaining its most influential adherents in cities like Antwerp, London, Amsterdam and Edinburgh, its chief appeal was to the new classes who engaged in trade and industry, and to whom the traditional scheme of social ethics seemed most out of date. The Calvinists recognised the necessity of capital, credit and banking, large-scale commerce and finance, and the other practical facts of business life. As Calvin himself put it, 'What reason is there why the income from business should not be larger than that from land-owning? Whence do the merchant's profits come from, except from his own diligence and industry?'[2]

Luther's idea of a calling as a fixed station in life thus began to give way to a new idea of a calling as a vocation to make good. Having been an obligation to remain in one's station, a person's calling now turned into an obligation to improve it. In due course, the calling turned into a drive to make money, and build up monetary wealth. As the Puritan divine, Richard Baxter, said, 'If God show you a way in which you may lawfully get more than in another way (without wrong to your soul or any other), if you refuse this and choose the less gainful way, you cross one of the ends of your calling, and you refuse to be God's steward, and to accept His gifts and use them for Him when He requireth it: you may labour to be rich for God, though not for the flesh and sin.'[3]

So the Puritan divines preached that, to be certain of your state of grace, you must do the works of Him who sent you as long as it is yet day. Unwillingness to work was a sure symptom of lack of grace. It was work, not leisure and enjoyment, that served to increase the glory of God. Wealthy and poor alike had a duty to work. Worldly work came to be seen as the purpose of life, ordained as such by God.

Attitudes to Time and Money

Most people in pre-industrial societies were aware of time as the rhythm of the natural world. Their clock was the sun and their calendars were the moon and the stars and the changing seasons. They managed their work accordingly. Only in places like cities and monasteries, where the rhythms of human life were distanced from the rhythms of nature, were other ways needed to mark the passage of time. The first people to live with careful measurement of time were, in fact, the medieval monks. They used church bells to help them to manage their time methodically in the service of God.

Methodicalness in the measurement and management of time became one of the two characteristic features of the industrial age. The other was a corresponding methodicalness in the measurement and management of value, i.e. the greatly enlarged part played by money in everyone's life.

> In the countryside this can be seen most clearly in the triumph of the money economy over the casual 'uneconomic' rhythms of peasant semi-subsistence. In the industrial areas it can be seen in the extension of the discipline of the factory bell or clock from working to leisure hours, from the working day to the Sabbath, and in the assault upon 'Cobbler's Monday' and traditional holidays and fairs.[4]

In the middle ages, monastic asceticism under such Catholic orders as the Benedictines, the Cistercians and the Jesuits had developed a systematic method of rational conduct, with the aim of freeing the monk from his own irrational impulses and his dependence on the world and nature. It trained him to work methodically in God's service and thereby to secure the salvation of his soul. This active and methodical self-control was taken over by the Puritans and re-directed towards activity within the world. 'Those passionately spiritual natures which had formerly supplied the highest type of monk, were now forced to pursue their ascetic ideals within mundane occupations.' In place of a spiritual aristocracy of monks outside and above the world, there was now a spiritual aristocracy of the predestined saints of God within the world.

> Christian asceticism, at first fleeing from the world into solitude, had already ruled the world (which it had renounced) from the monastery and through the Church. But it had, on the whole, left the naturally spontaneous character of daily life in the world untouched. Now it strode into the market-place of life, slammed the door of the monastery behind it, and undertook to penetrate just that daily routine of life with its methodicalness.[5]

So the Puritan divines laid great stress on the value of time. Waste of time, for the puritan conscience, became the first and deadliest of sins. Life was all too short; there was little time to make sure of one's own salvation; to waste such time as one had was a sin: 'Those that are prodigal of their time despise their own souls.' Even contemplation was valueless if it was at the expense of one's daily work and the active performance of

God's will in one's calling. Richard Baxter exhorted his listeners to 'Keep up a high esteem of time, and be every day more careful that you lose none of your time than you are that you lose none of your gold and silver.' Benjamin Franklin went one step further, asking his readers to 'remember that time is money. He that idly loses five shillings worth of time loses five shillings, and might as prudently throw five shillings into the sea'. The idea that every hour lost was an hour lost to labour for the glory of God, was transformed into the idea that every hour lost was an hour lost to the making of money.

Thus the shift from the earlier qualitative awareness of time in tune with the earth's diurnal and seasonal rhythms, that characterised pre-industrial ways of life, to the later obsession with quantitative time that has characterised the industrial age, paralleled and reinforced the comparable shift in people's understanding and awareness of value. Whereas in pre-industrial times the value of most things, including work, was qualitatively experienced in the satisfaction of needs, the inhabitants of late industrial societies have become obsessed with the money value of everything, including work. The effect of the Cartesian split, in this as in other spheres, has been to exalt quantitative calculation at the expense of qualitative experience.[6]

A Work Ethic for All

After the Reformation there was a much greater gulf between the predestined Puritan elect and the damned remainder of humanity than there had been between medieval monks and the society around them. Conscious of divine grace, the Puritan elect had little sympathy for their sinful neighbours, but hated and despised them as enemies of God condemned to eternal damnation. This harshness towards the less fortunate was reflected in harsher policies towards the poor.

In the middle ages, as Tawney says, 'popular feeling had lent a half-mystical glamour to proverty and to the compassion by which poverty was relieved, for poor men were God's friends'. Latimer had preached that 'the poor man hath title to the rich man's goods; so that the rich man ought to let the poor man have part of his riches to help and to comfort him withal'. But now it was a different story:

That the greatest of evils is idleness, that the poor are the vic-
tims, not of circumstances, but of their own idle, irregular and
wicked courses, that the truest charity is not to enervate them
by relief, but so to reform their characters that relief may be
unnecessary – such doctrines turned severity from a sin into a
duty and froze the impulse of natural pity with the assurance
that, if indulged, it would perpetuate the suffering which it
sought to allay.[7]

In short, with the Protestant Reformation came the view that
the elect should insist on work, not only for themselves, but
also for the poor. In England an Act of Parliament was passed
in 1649 for the relief and employment of the poor and the
punishment of beggars, under which a company was to be
established with power to apprehend vagrants, to offer them
the choice between work and whipping, and to set to compulsory labour all other poor persons, including children,
without means of maintenance. Milton's friend Hartlib
expressed the mood of the times: 'The law of God saith, "He
that will not work, let him not eat." This would be a sore
scourge and smart whip for idle persons if none should be suffered to eat till they had wrought for it.'

Meanwhile, against this background of harshness towards
what would later become the working class, Puritan divines
like Baxter were developing the concept of a calling into a
regular specialised job. 'Outside of a well-marked calling the
accomplishments of a man are only casual and irregular, and
he spends more time in idleness than in work ... (The
specialised worker) will carry out his work in order, while
another remains in constant confusion and his work knows
neither time nor place ... Therefore is a certain calling the
best for everyone.' Baxter also anticipated Adam Smith by
more than 100 years in pointing to the division of labour as the
source of improvement in production and economic growth.[8]

Thus, on the one hand the Puritan ethic justified the profit-
making business activities of the employer as a sign that he was
among the elect, while on the other the ethical importance
(later strengthened by Methodism) of a fixed calling and
unremitting work, justified regular, specialised work for the
employee.

A specifically bourgeois economic ethic had grown up, With the consciousness of standing in the fullness of God's grace and being visibly blessed by Him, the bourgeois businessman. . . could follow his pecuniary interests as he would and feel that he was fulfilling a duty in doing so. The power of religious asceticism provided him in addition with sober, conscientious, and usually industrious workmen, who clung to their work as to a life purpose willed by God.

On the one hand, the religious conversion of large numbers of working-class people to the Protestant work ethic undermined their resistance to exploitation and was thus against their own best interest. On the other, the Protestant bourgeois work ethic in due course brought forth working-class consciousness in opposition to itself. But the centrally relevant fact for us, thinking about the future of work today, is that from the Protestant work ethic stemmed the basis on which work in late industrial societies has been organised, that is the assumption that work means employment and that every normal adult of working age should have a job. The crucial point is that this new work ethic, shaped by the experience and perspectives of a non-conformist minority in the middle ranks of society, provided the form of work that eventually dominated society as a whole. In shaping a new work ethic for the post-industrial age, will non-conforming people from the middle ranks of society today have a comparable part to play?

Change as Liberation and Progress
Medieval society was hierarchical and, for the most part, rigid and static. God was understood to have placed people in their respective ranks; the monarch, together with lords and prelates, high and mighty, was at the top; the poor and lowly were at the bottom; and everyone else was on rungs of the ladder in between. Only in exceptional cases would someone move up or down. This social order was thought of as remaining unchanged. It reflected the medieval perception of the universe as hierarchical and static, with God at the top with his court of archangels, then the angels, then humans (a little lower than the angels and a little higher than the beasts), then the beasts, then plants, and so on down the full range of God's creation. Work in such a society and such a universe was the

work required of you by your place in it. It was governed by
the obligations attaching to your place – for example, the
obligations of the peasant to his lord, and vice versa. Most
men and women unquestioningly took up the same work as
their parents, as successive generations followed in the
footsteps of those who went before.

Industrial society, by contrast, has been more flexible and
evolving. Relaxation of the medieval obligations which kept
people in their place brought more freedom of movement,
and those who could grasp the opportunities this gave began
to see work as a way of bettering themselves. For those who
thus experienced the coming of industrial society as opening
new dimensions of freedom, its evolution was perceived as
progress. In fact, the dominant ethos of 19th-century Britain
was an ethos of progress – the progress of science and industry
in harnessing the resources of the natural world to human use,
and the progress of imperial power in bringing European
civilisation, the pax Britannica, and the Christian religion to
'lesser breeds without the law'. The middle-class outlook of
that time saw work as a contribution to progress in these senses,
and many middle-class people dedicated themselves to their
work for that reason as well as for more selfish ones.

There was, however, the other side of the coin. As the old
obligations of social superiors to social inferiors crumbled,
the new mobility had disastrous effects on many people,
especially in the lower ranges of society. As they were pushed
down the ladder they suffered deprivation, injustice, and loss
of self-respect. Those on whom the evolution of industrial
society imposed new dimensions, not of freedom, but of
necessity, experienced it as the reverse of liberation and progress. They came to perceive work as something that they, in
their position in society, were forced to do for other people
better placed than themselves. The prevailing working-class
attitude to work became very different from the dominant
attitude based on the outlook of the more fortunate middle
classes. We shall return to this in Chapter 8.

Work Ethic or Leisure Ethic?

The Protestant work ethic took a particular historical form,
which subsequently developed into the formalised version
which dominates late industrial societies today. Strictly speak-

ing, this is now an employment, or job, ethic, rather than a work ethic in the true sense. Most people believe they *ought* to have a job and try to get one and keep one, but the majority of people *in* jobs are probably not very deeply committed to their work. The true work ethic is now more likely to be found among self-employed people and others who have decided not to work in a conventional job, but rather to dedicate themselves wholeheartedly to their own chosen sphere of work, than among employees. It is based on the perception that work is a good and valuable activity for what it achieves. It is perceived as activity that meets needs – other people's as well as the worker's – and, in meeting those needs, brings with it a sense of self-esteem and (in most cases) social belonging. People who subscribe to the work ethic see work as activity that gives meaning to their lives and brings opportunity for their own development and self-fulfilment.

Such people may perceive work, as did the medieval Benedictine monks, as a way of offering their life in worship and prayer to God; or, as other Christians have seen it, as a way of taking part in God's creation, as co-creators with God. This Christian view of work has been powerfully reaffirmed in recent years:

> Through work man must earn his daily bread and contribute to the continual advance of science and technology and, above all, to elevating unceasingly the cultural and moral level of the society within which he lives in community with those who belong to the same family. And work means any activity by man, whether manual or intellectual, whatever its nature or circumstances; it means any human activity that can and must be recognised as work, in the midst of all the many activities of which man is capable and to which he is predisposed by his very nature, by virtue of humanity itself. Man is made to be in the visible universe an image and likeness of God himself, and he is placed in it in order to subdue the Earth. From the beginning therefore he is called to work. Work is one of the characteristics that distinguish man from the rest of creatures, whose activity for sustaining their lives cannot be called work.[9]

These are the opening words of the Encyclical Letter, *Laborem Exercens*, of Pope John Paul II, published in 1981. I personally doubt whether the purpose of human life is to 'subdue the earth'; and I see the sharp distinction between humans and other creatures as a survival from a hierarchical worldview which is on the way out. Nonetheless, the work ethic is powerfully affirmed: work is activity that contributes to the purposes of life; if you think your life has (or should have) any purpose beyond the mere living of it, your work will be (or should be) activity that contributes to that purpose; therefore your work will have (or should have) some kind of spiritual significance for you.

Marxists agree with Christians that work is the central activity of human life which distinguishes humans from other creatures such as ants and bees. But whereas Christians perceive human work as a process of co-creation with God, Marx saw it as a process whereby human beings create themselves and, increasingly, the world around them:

> Labour is, first of all, a process between man and nature, a process by which man, through his own actions, mediates, regulates and controls the metabolism between himself and nature. He confronts the materials of nature as a force of nature. He sets in motion the natural forces which belong to his own body, his arms, legs, head and hands, in order to appropriate the materials of nature in a form adapted to his own needs. Through this movement he acts upon external nature and changes it, and in this way he simultaneously changes his own nature.[10]

Work, for Marx, was the process of human self-création.

There is also a more ecological view of the centrality of work to human life. In contrast to the Christian and Marxist views, this sees working as participating in the processes of nature, rather than subduing and changing them. As Khalil Gibran puts it: 'You work that you may keep pace with the earth and the soul of the earth. For to be idle is to become a stranger unto the seasons, and to step out of life's procession that marches in majesty towards the infinite. To love life through labour is to be intimate with life's inmost secret.'[11]

Among those who have subscribed to the work ethic are many who have drawn attention to the distinction between good work and bad. For example, while the dominant strand in Christian thinking about work sees it as a blessing, another strand sees work as an unavoidable curse laid on humanity by

God as punishment for Adam's original sin. William Morris echoed this distinction when he defined work as being of two kinds, 'one good, the other bad; one not far removed from a blessing, a lightening of life; the other a mere curse, a burden to life. . . . Worthy work carries with it the hope of pleasure in rest, the hope of pleasure in using what it makes, and the hope of pleasure in our daily creative skill. All other work but this is worthless; it is slaves' work – mere toiling to live that we may live to toil'.[12]

E. F. Schumacher similarly contrasted good work with bad. An example of bad work, he said, is the mindless repetitive boredom of working on a factory assembly line, which destroys initiative and rots brains. Good work, by contrast, is that which achieves the three main purposes of human work: first, to provide necessary and useful goods and services; second, to enable every one of us to use and thereby perfect our gifts like good stewards; third, to do so in service to, and in co-operation with, others, so as to liberate ourselves from our inborn egocentricity. Schumacher went on to say that 'this threefold function makes work so central to human life that it is truly impossible to conceive of life at the human level without work'. And then he quoted Albert Camus: 'Without work, all life goes rotten. But when work is soulless, life stifles and dies.'[13]

Awareness that work can often be bad may lead people to discard the work ethic altogether and replace it by a leisure ethic. Bertrand Russell, for example, distinguished between two kinds of work, as follows:'First, altering the position of matter at or near the earth's surface relatively to such other matter; second, telling other people to do so. The first kind is unpleasant and ill-paid, the second is pleasant and highly paid.' In fact, Russell was making several distinctions here: apart from those between pleasant and unpleasant, and well-paid and ill-paid work, there were the distinctions between the work of subordinates and the work of superiors, and between physical and non-physical work. But the important point is that, in contrast to Morris and Schumacher who were concerned with 'useful' work and 'good' work, Russell was writing 'in praise of idleness'.[14] Whereas Morris and Schumacher both thought work was essentially good, the aristocratic Russell thought work essentially something to be avoided.

Whereas, in general, the people in the middling ranks of society tend to subscribe to a work ethic, those at either end of the social spectrum are more likely to rate leisure higher than work. Aristocrats are inclined to think of work, as the ancient Greeks and Romans did, as something to be done by inferiors and slaves and to be avoided by self-respecting citizens; and courtiers, playboys, rentiers and financiers have always tended to think of work as something which less fortunate or less intelligent people should be persuaded or cajoled into carrying out on their behalf. At the same time, the poorer sections of society have often been inclined to agree with Snoopy that 'work is the crab-grass in the lawn of life', to be cut to the minimum if not rooted out altogether. They have tended to feel that 'if work were a good thing, the rich would have found a way to keep it to themselves'.[15]

A question for the future, then, is whether a leisure eithic or a revived work ethic is more likely to prevail. Those who support a HE future in which most people will live lives of leisure, believe that a leisure ethic will be one of its most important features. On the other hand those who support a SHE future in which ownwork will play a growing part in many people's lives, believe that a new work ethic will be central to it.

Meanwhile, the third, Business As Usual, view believes that work in the form of employment, though often having little value in itself, will continue to be necessary for instrumental reasons – as a means of earning a livelihood or achieving some other desirable end. Some may welcome that kind of work as an opiate, as a means of enabling them to forget or ignore the anxieties, miseries or meaninglessness of their lives. Many workaholics regard work in this way. Voltaire, at the end of *Candide*, expressed it thus: 'Work wards off three great evils: boredom, vice and poverty . . . Let us work, then, and not argue. It is the only way to make life bearable.' Many young people will no doubt continue to perceive a job as what initiates them into adulthood and enables them to escape from the narrow confines of their family into the wider world. Many men, and many women, may still see comparatively orderly routine jobs in factories, offices and the like as a means of at least temporary escape from the anxieties, traumas and muddles of children, housework, and family life. Traditional supporters of law and order will continue to favour work – for

other people, that is – not so much for its own sake as because
they think the Devil finds mischief for idle hands to do.

A New Work Ethic

These different views about work and leisure will all exist in
the future as in the past. Different people will continue to have
different attitudes. Some people will be responsible and hard-
working, others will be irresponsible and lazy. Some will be
ambitious, others easily contented. Some will be conscientious, others happy-go-lucky. Some will see work as a good
thing, to be welcomed with enthusiasm. Some will see it as a
bad thing, to be avoided whenever possible. Some will take a
more neutral view, accepting work as a fact of life, and trying to
make the best of it. These differences will simply reflect the
fact that different people have different physical and mental
capacities, different temperaments, different opportunities,
different experiences, different positions in society, and different cultural backgrounds.

But, overriding these differences of outlook between different people, a new work ethic will almost certainly emerge. It
is likely to be more powerful than either the existing job ethic
or whatever leisure ethic may develop, reflecting the fact that
the development of ownwork will have a deeper impact on the
way people live and organise themselves, and will be a more
important factor in shaping the future, than either the continuing existence of employment as a form of work or the
expansion of leisure.

The new work ethic will be based, as was the Protestant work
ethic when it was new, on a fresh perception of reality. Increasing numbers of people are already beginning to perceive that
real life is not to be found in the formalised activities of business, government and money. In late industrial societies these
have become overdeveloped to a point where they treat
people, not as real people, but as organisational abstractions
like employees, customers, managers, pensioners, and so on.
Real life is rather to be found in the informal spheres of
activity where people confront themselves and one another as
real people. Just as the Lutheran ethic taught that worldly
work was more real than withdrawal into the artificial, abstracted
sphere of ecclesiastical life, so the new work ethic now will

teach that to immerse oneself in today's organisational world is to sink into a world of abstractions and turn one's back on real life; and that real life means real experience, and real work means finding ways of acting directly to meet needs – one's own, other people's and, increasingly, the survival needs of the natural world which supports us.

The direction in which the new work ethic will lead us will, however, differ in vital respects from that which the Protestant ethic opened up. For example, the Protestant ethic emphasised quantitative values, as in its new concern with money and time, and it placed great weight on individualism and the impersonal approach. In these and other respects it reflected the new worldview that was taking shape at that time. As we shall see in the next two chapters, the pendulum now has begun to swing the other way. This will profoundly affect our work ethic and the way we value such things as money and time.

However, there are two important features which the emergence of the new work ethic today will have in common with the emergence of the Protestant work ethic in its time.

First, as we noted earlier, the Protestant work ethic was pioneered by a non-conforming minority from the middle range of society, who turned away from the old ways of doing and thinking and opened up new ways. The same thing is beginning to happen today as non-conforming minorities, mainly of middle-class people, turn away from the old orthodoxies of the industrial age and begin to open up new, saner, more humane, more ecological ways of doing and thinking. The differences are, of course, profound. Today's pioneers are not, in the main, individualists, obsessed with the question of their own individual salvation. On the contrary, they are powerfully moved by the prospect of a richer personal and spiritual life which community participation seems to offer, and which the conventional way of life in industrialised society largely precludes. Nor do they make the harsh distinction between themselves as elect and other people as damned that their Puritan predecessors made. They know that, if humankind is to change direction and set out on a new path of progress, this must be an enterprise in which everyone has an opportunity to share.

The second point in common is that the new work ethic will

mean a great liberation of human energies into new and useful activities, just as the Protestant ethic did in its time. But whereas then liberation for some was at the expense of lost freedom for others, this time it will be possible for all to share in liberation from the forms of dependency now imposed by being employed, or not, as the case may be. The only freedom that will be lost will be the freedom to exploit other people and keep them dependent. Whereas the Protestant work ethic could be used to keep the many dependent on the few and to compel the many to work for the few, the new work ethic will be based on the principle of enabling all people to become more self-reliant.[16]

Changing Worldview,
Changing Values

The Industrial-Age Outlook
In the middle ages people perceived themselves as belonging organically to a natural and social order which was divinely sanctioned, hierarchical and unchanging. They worked, and perceived their work, accordingly. Their outlook was personal. They thought of God as a separate, supremely powerful person, who had brought them into existence as part of his creation and was able either to condemn them to everlasting punishment or to raise them to perpetual bliss. They thought of their social and economic relations as relations between people, and saw society as consisting of persons and being governed by particular persons. It is true that medieval religious culture had attempted with fair success to depersonalise mountains, rivers, trees, houses and other places which earlier pagan cultures had identified with living spirits. But, nonetheless, people perceived themselves as having been given their own particular place as human beings a little lower than the angels and a little above the beasts, in the predominantly personal world of God's creation.

The Renaissance, the Protestant Reformation and, ultimately, the industrial revolution brought a complete change of outlook. We distanced ourselves from the natural universe around us and came to regard ourselves as separate from it. Since then, from a position outside nature, we have measured it and studied it, exploited it and harnessed it. We have treated nature as an object in relation to ourselves, by bringing to bear upon it the objective processes of science and the manipulative processes of technology. We have regarded nature as a machine, to be understood and explained from outside by natural scientists, and to be worked from outside by engineers, industrialists and factory farmers. We have treated other species as things, to be captured, observed, vivisected, used and destroyed to suit human purposes. This perception of nature as something apart from ourselves has had a tremendous impact on what we have thought of as work, and on the kinds of work people have done and have valued during the industrial age.

Similarly, we learned to distance ourselves from other people and society. We learned to think of ourselves as separate individuals and of other people as impersonal role-players, like consumers and employees. We learned to think of society as a machine. We learned to suppose that people and society could be understood by observation from outside by economists, market researchers, political scientists, and other social scientists; and we learned to suppose that they could be manipulated by intervention from outside by businessmen and politicians. One result is that many people's work today is concerned with observing people at a distance and dealing with them impersonally as consumers, employees, voters, pensioners, housewives, social welfare clients, viewers, and so on.

The industrial age has also taught us to distance ourselves from ourselves. For example, it has taught us to think of our bodies as machines, to be understood and manipulated by observation and intervention from outside – as in the diagnoses and treatments of conventional medicine. This conceptual model of ourselves in relation to our bodies reflected the Cartesian duality, and led us to think of ourselves as a 'mind in a machine'. Then, as psychologists taught us that our minds too can be manipulated from outside by drugs and other interventionist treatments, we came to perceive ourselves as separate, not just from our bodies, but also from our minds. So, in our work, we came to use our bodies, and then our minds, as instruments of work – as if the physical work done by our bodies and the brainwork done by our minds could be distanced from our real selves. The growing separation between work and what many people perceived as their real life, paralleled this growing separation of ourselves from our bodies and our minds.

Finally, the medieval concept of the divine as a person gave way to a dominant concept of the universe as a vast impersonal machine: 'Man at last knows that he is alone in the unfeeling immensity of the universe, out of which he emerged only by chance.'[1]

The medieval universe, and the medieval social order, was assumed to enjoy a stability that was morally sanctioned by a personal God. The removal of those moral sanctions brought new perceptions of freedom, both to act and to be acted upon. The perception that one could be a subject, or an object, or both, became much sharper. People came to see themselves, as active subjects in relation to the natural world, which they increasingly perceived as the impersonal and mechanistic object of their actions. In relation to other people they saw themselves no longer as co-existing in the position in the social order in which God had placed them, but as either subject or object – either, from a more powerful position in society, acting upon other people and directing or manipulating them, or, from a less powerful position, being acted upon and directed and manipulated by them. To begin with this was reflected in new personal relationships between masters and men. Then, as the structures of later industrialised society became increasingly depersonalised, people came to see themselves either as helping to operate the mechanisms of business, government, finance and other component parts of the society machine, or as being acted upon and manipulated by these mechanisms. The first attitude is part of the outlook of the managerial and professional classes, the second an aspect of working-class consciousness. In either case, the effect on people's perception of work has been profound.

A Post-Industrial Worldview

There are already signs that the post-industrial worldview may be fundamentally different in many ways.

A sign of our changing perception of our relationship with nature is the upsurge of concern in recent years about the countryside, the way we treat other living creatures and the land, our destruction of species (of plants as well as animals), the threat to the tropical forests, desertification, pollution, the exhaustion of the Earth's natural resources, and so on. The outlook of many of the environmentalists who voice these concerns is still, perhaps, largely mechanistic. They perceive planet Earth as a machine which we may be in danger of running into the ground. But, there are other signs that a more truly ecological attitude to nature is taking firm root.

For example, scientists are beginning to discuss the 'Gaia hypothesis'.[2] They are discovering that the entire range of living matter on Earth, including the human species, can be regarded as a single living entity, capable of manipulating the Earth's atmosphere to suit its overall needs and endowed with faculties and powers far beyond those of its constituent parts. This has already proved a valuable hypothesis to scientists, and has suggested experimental questions and answers which have been scientifically fruitful. Another example is the revival of interest, especially in North America, in the traditional North American Indian attitude to the natural world. Chief Seattle's oration of 1852 speaks to us today: 'This we know. The earth does not belong to man; man belongs to the earth. This we know. All things are connected. Whatever befalls the earth, befalls the sons of the earth. Man did not weave the web of life. He is merely a strand in it. Whatever he does to the web, he does to himself.'[3] Yet another example is the discovery of modern physicists that the universe has to be 'experienced as a dynamic, inseparable whole, which always includes the observer in an essential way'.[4] Emphasis is now beginning to shift from consciousness of being apart from nature to consciousness of being a part of it; from external observation to direct experience; from instrumental intervention to direct involvement. If this shift of emphasis continues, it is bound to have a powerful effect on the values we give to different kinds of work.

Something very similar is beginning to happen to our perceptions of society. For example, 'barefoot economists' are beginning to live in communities, helping to animate local self-development from within.[5] This contrasts sharply with the work of conventional economists, who manipulate statistical aggregates and impersonal instruments of policy from outside. In the sphere of politics, local participatory politics is spreading as a response to the inadequacies of representative national politics carried out by professional politicians at a remove.[6] In general, the idea is gaining ground that the best way to help people is by working *with* them, not *on* them or *for* them; and that the best way to understand society and to change it is from within, by living the change and being personally part of it ourselves. In short, direct involvement is coming to be seen as a more effective approach to social change than trying to manipulate change by political and economic intervention from outside. This too is bound to have a powerful effect on the values we attach to different kinds of work.

There are comparable signs that the post-industrial transition will also bring a more holistic perception of ourselves. 'Holistic health', 'alternative therapies' and 'humanistic psychology' are some of many new approaches which are beginning to treat body, mind and spirit as a unity. 'Transpersonal psychology' and 'psycho-synthesis' are two of many new disciplines that aim to teach us to integrate ourselves.[7] This new perspective on personal health and development is likely to affect increasingly the kinds of work we value, and the kinds of work we are prepared to set our bodies and minds to do.

Finally, it seems that a comparable change is already beginning to affect our perceptions of the supernatural and the divine, and that the concept of a pitiless impersonal cosmos from which we are excluded may well be replaced by that of an evolving superpersonal universe of which we ourselves are part. Gaia is one way of describing this. Teilhard de Chardin's cosmogenesis is another.[8] As the 'consciousness revolution'[9] encourages increasing numbers of people to cultivate the experience, well-known to mystics through the ages, of being in a state of oneness with the cosmos, a new perception of the divine is beginning to crystallise as an evolving collective consciousness which we ourselves help to create, by the way we live our lives and develop our own potential. This brings together the Christian concept of human beings as co-creators of the world with God, and the Marxist concept of human beings as creators of themselves and the world. It will powerfully affect the way we think about the purposes of life and work, and the kinds of work we value.

The post-industrial universe and the post-industrial social order thus seem likely to be experienced not as hierarchical or fixed or as morally sanctioned by an external personal God, as in the middle ages; nor as a competitive arena in which one has either to act or to be acted upon, as in the industrial age. A more ecological understanding of our relations with other species and the natural world will mean our seeing ourselves as co-existing with them 'as part of the same web', rather than seeing them merely as potential objects of our actions. Similarly, we shall tend to perceive society as a web of social relationships in which each person interacts to a greater or lesser degree with each, and no longer as a machine that enables some to act upon others. The important purposes of work will then be seen, not as finding new ways of taming the natural world and exploiting it for our own use,[10] but as creating permanently sustainable ways to live in harmony with it; and not as achieving economic or social or political success at the expense of our fellow humans, but as finding ways to ensure that the free development of ourselves will contribute to the free development of our fellows, and vice versa.

Shifting Values
There is now a fair amount of evidence that some such shift of values as I have been outlining has begun to take place in the industrialised world over the last 20 years. It has been most intensively studied in the United States, but the same broad pattern of change seems to hold good for other countries, too.

The Stanford Research Institute (SRI) has for many years been looking at American values in the context of business marketing. Three of their main categories for consumers are: 'need-driven', 'outer-directed', and 'inner-directed'. The consumption habits of the need-driven are determined by their need for basics and their lack of money; those of the outer-directed are determined by their need to belong, to emulate the trend-setters, and to be seen as achievers; and those of the inner-directed are determined by their need to express themselves, to experience and participate, and to be socially conscious – for example, by supporting 'such causes as conservation, environmentalism and consumerism'. (A fourth category, 'integrated', is for the 'rare people who have it all together. They wield the power of outer-directedness with the sensitivity of inner-directedness'. But there are not many of these paragons and they cannot be identified empirically!)[11]

An important finding of these studies is that a shift is taking place from outer-directed to inner-directed values. The following lists are presented to suggest the nature of this shift:

Past Symbols of Success
Fame
Being in *Who's Who*
Five-Figure Salary
College Degree
Splendid Home
Executive Position
Live-in Servants
New Car Every Year

Present Symbols of Success
Unlisted Phone Number
Swiss Bank Account
Connections with Celebrities
Deskless Office
Second and Third Home
Being a Vice President
Being Published
Frequent World Travel

Future Symbols of Success
Free Time Any Time
Recognition as a Creative Person
Oneness of Work and Play
Rewarded less by Money than by Respect and Affection
Major Societal Commitments
Easy Laughter, Unembarrassed Tears
Philosophical Independence
Loving, and In Touch with Self

The message is reasonably clear, even if the focus on *symbols of success* suggests that the people by whom and for whom these studies were carried out may not yet have shaken off outer-directed values!

In his recent book,[12] Duane Elgin (formerly a researcher at SRI) discusses the 'whole pattern of practical changes that a growing number of people are making in their lives . . . This innovative way of living is termed Voluntary Simplicity'. Elgin estimates that some ten million people in the United States were wholeheartedly exploring a life of voluntary simplicity in

1980, and that this could well 'become the dominant orien-
tation for the majority of the adult population of many Western developed nations by the year 2000'. The emerging
system of values associated with voluntary simplicity, which
Elgin contrasts with the industrial value system, is very similar
to the value system implied by the SHE vision of the future (see
Chapter 1).

In another recent book Daniel Yankelovich, of the American
opinion-polling firm of Yankelovich, Skelly and White, con-
firms this shift away from (in his terms) instrumental,
materialistic, technological, self-denying values to values centred
around self-fulfilment. The new values, he says, are based on
the need for activities that have value in their own right and on
the idea that people have value in themselves. In an even more
recent report on 'Work and Human Values' of which
Yankelovich was one of the authors, this emerging new value
system is called 'expressivism' (corresponding to 'inner-
directed') in contrast to 'material success' (corresponding to
'outer-directed'). The five core values of expressivism are described as:

(1) emphasis on inner growth rather than on external signs
    of success;
(2) living in harmony with nature;
(3) autonomy, as opposed to dependence on authority;
(4) hedonism;
(5) community. [13]

So far as the more fortunate groups in society are concerned
this shift in values was no doubt prompted at first by the
experience of material security. In the United States of the
1960s, the young people – who are today's middle-aged – were
the post-scarcity generation. They took for granted that their
material needs would be met, and their aspirations shifted to
the non-material aspects of life. However, in the 1970s the
limits to conventional economic expansion began to close in,
and it was not long before the industrialised world, including
the United States, faced the prospect of neo-scarcity. Assuming that the shift from the old technological, materialist values
to the new ecological, non-materialist values continues, this
will be only partly because the new approach has come to

seem desirable. It will also be partly because it has come to be accepted as necessary.

This shift of values will probably continue. But the process is likely to be confused. There could be increasing diversity in the values and aspirations of different persons, different groups and – to some extent – different countries. For one thing, development of a greater variety of communications media will help to show people many different possible life-styles, in contrast to the dominant set of standards communicated by the mass communications of the mass consumption society. On the other hand, if economic and employment prospects continue depressed, the revival of material priorities such as having a well-paid job and the consumer lifestyle that goes with it, which has been evident in some sections of the population in, for example, Reagan's America and Thatcher's Britain in the last few years, could continue. There could thus be an increasing polarisation of value systems and a sharper division between those who hold to the old technological, materialist values and those who do not. This would be reflected in deepening disagreement about the value of work in general and about the relative value of work of different kinds.

Masculine And Feminine

One of the most important components of the shift that is now taking place from the old value system to a new one is the shift from masculine to feminine values. More people are coming to perceive the present human crisis – the arms race, third world poverty, exhaustion of natural resources, destruction and pollution of the biosphere, mass unemployment, diseases of civilisation, and so on – as a crisis of masculine values. More people are realising that the industrial age has been a very masculine age, and that this is a source of many problems now.

Thanks to Jung and other psychologists, it is now widely accepted and understood that within each one of us, whether we are men or women, there is both a masculine and a feminine side. This duality must be kept in balance if we are to be a full person, whole, healthy and fulfilled, and capable of functioning well. A man whose feminine side is suppressed and undeveloped and altogether subordinated to his masculine side as he struggles his way through the stressful world of telegrams and anger, will find himself arid and unfilfilled when eventually the mid-life crisis hits him and he wonders what it's all for. And the woman whose masculine side is correspondingly undeveloped may find that she is unable to organise herself to cope with the practicalities of life in a largely man-made world.

This masculine/feminine polarity can be found in societies, too. According to Erich Fromm in *The Sane Society*,[14] a patriarchal society is characterised by respect for man-made law, by rational thought, and by sustained efforts to control and change the natural world; whereas a matriarchal society is characterised by the importance of blood ties, close links with the land, and acceptance of human dependence on nature. Patriarchy attaches high value to order and authority, obedience and hierarchy; whereas matriarchy lays stress on love, unity and universal harmony. The healthy society is one in which both the masculine and feminine principles are developed and in balance with one another.

Late industrial society has become so unhealthy in this respect, the masculine and the feminine have split so far apart, and the masculine has come to dominate the feminine so much, that it is hardly too much to feel that we now live in a nightmare fantasy world. The nightmare is all too real; the outcome could be the nuclear holocaust.

In *The Imperial Animal* Lionel Tiger and Robin Fox describe the nature of the fantasy. Human males have:

> all the enthusiasms of the hunting primate, but few of the circumstances in which this reality can be reflected. So they create their own realities; they make up teams; they set up businesses and political parties; they form secret societies and cabals for and against the government; they set up regiments; they make up fantasies about honour and dignity; they turn their enemies into 'not men', into prey. They generate forms of automatic loyalty and complete dedication than can spread the Jesuitical message of the Church Militant and also send screaming jets to a foreign country. All a country needs is a couple of dozen males who take their fantasies about their own omnipotence so seriously that they spend money, kill people, and even commit Abraham's presumptuous conceit of sacrificing their sons to voices of grandeur they think they hear.[15]

Meanwhile, as Virginia Woolf pointed out in *A Room of One's Own*, the human female has aided and abetted the human male in these dangerous fantasies:

> Women have served all these centuries as looking-glasses possessing the magic and delicious power of reflecting the figure of man at twice its natural size. Without that power, probably the earth would still be swamp and jungle. The glories of all our wars would be unknown . . . Mirrors are essential to all violent and heroic action. That is why Napoleon and Mussolini insist so emphatically upon the inferiority of women, for if they were not inferior they would cease to enlarge . . . How is a man to go on giving judgement, civilizing natives, making law, writing books, dressing up and speechifying at banquets, unless he can see himself at breakfast and dinner at least twice the size he really is? . . . The looking-glass vision is of extreme importance because it charges the vitality; it stimulates the nervous system. Take it away and men may die, like the drug fiend deprived of his cocaine.[16]

How is this split between the masculine and the feminine to be healed? How is a more androgynous balance to be created? In the rest of this chapter we shall explore these questions in the context of the future of men's work and women's work.

Men's Work and Women's Work

In every society in the past it seems that the tasks done by men and the tasks done by women have been clearly distinguished from each other. Here, for example, is an account of the bushmen of Southern Africa at work:

> A woman gathers on one day enough food to feed her family for three days, and spends the rest of her time resting in camp, doing embroidery, visiting other camps, or entertaining visitors from other camps. For each day at home, kitchen routines, such as cooking, nut cracking, collecting firewood and fetching water, occupy one to three hours of her time. This rhythm of steady work and steady leisure is maintained throughout the year. The hunters tend to work more frequently than the women but their schedule is uneven. It is not unusual for a man to hunt avidly for a week and then do no hunting at all for two or three weeks. Since hunting is an unpredictable business and subject to magical control, hun-

ters sometimes experience a run of bad luck and stop hunting for a month or longer. During these periods, visiting, entertaining, and especially dancing are the primary activities of men.[17]

In pre-industrial Europe, too, there was a clear division of labour between women and men in traditional rural areas.[18] Everywhere the pattern seems to have been much the same. Inside the house, women were responsible for child-rearing, cooking, cleaning, and for cottage-industrial tasks like spinning, knitting, glove-stitching and lace-making, whereas the only indoor task for men apart from house construction and repair seems to have been lighting the oven. Outside the house, women were responsible for wood-gleaning, water-carrying, vegetable-growing, weeding, and poultry and dairy work, whereas men were responsible for digging, ploughing, scything, slaughtering, and cattle-marketing. Whereas men were responsible for managing the farm and doing the farm accounts, women were responsible for managing the household. These sex roles were absolute and had to be strictly observed. The community punished with ridicule those who attempted to break them down. A husband who milked the cows, carried water or washed dishes would become a local laughing-stock. Men and women each had their own station, laid down by custom and tradition, and they were not expected to work outside it. In this, the situation in the household reflected the organisation of work in society as a whole.

Within their own particular domain women had a great deal of power to manage their tasks without men's interference. Nonetheless, it seems to have been the case in most societies that men's work role and status came to be considered superior to women's. Edward Shorter describes how 'the systematic subordination of women by peasant men that we commonly encounter' in pre-industrial Europe was sanctified by the rituals of daily life. For example, wives did not join their husbands at meals, but waited on them.

In the pre-industrial household, then, as in society as a whole, the organisation of work seems to have reflected the distribution of power and status. Just as masters were more powerful than slaves, and lords than serfs, in society as a whole, so men's status was higher than women's in the household. It is arguable how far this was a question of physical strength. It is certainly true that strength was a powerful asset in pre-industrial conditions, and also that many husbands could exercise physical force over their wives. But the superiority of men's work status also reflected the fact that they were responsible for paying taxes and rents, and for dealing with officialdom. They were head of their household in the eyes of the world. Responsibility for their households' links with the outside world also meant they had to spend time in the local tavern, sitting around and drinking with their friends. In pre-industrial, as in industrial, times men tended to have more leisure than women.

The fact that men were primarily responsible for relations between their households and the world outside, and especially for their monetary relations with it, meant that, when subsistence work gave place to wage labour and when, as the industrial age came in, employment became the dominant form of work, it was natural for the man of the household to slip into the role of wage-earner and breadwinner. So the gap in status between men's work and women's work widened further. Women's roles may have already been seen as subservient to men's in some respects, but now the unpaid work of women inside the home was seen as merely ancillary to the paid work of men in the world outside.[19]

This widening gap in status between the work thought typical of men and the work thought typical of women was symptomatic of the growing dominance of the masculine over the feminine in post-medieval life and thought. The outlook of medieval society may have had a masculine bias, as we have seen, but the importance of the feminine was at least recognised; witness the status given to the Virgin Mary in medieval Catholic theology alongside the masculine Trinity of God the Father, God the Son, and God the Holy Ghost. After the Reformation, Protestant thinking swept even that aside, as an increasingly masculine society reshaped its theology to reflect its values.

Equal Opportunities
The downgrading of women's work in comparison with men's was directly connected with the central change in the organisation of work that came in with the industrial age – that is, the

downgrading of unpaid, informal work (which remained the typical province of women) in comparison with paid work in formal employment (which became the typical province of men).

From this it has followed naturally that, when women subsequently began to campaign for more equal rights and opportunities with men in the sphere of work, they concentrated on improving the position of women in formal employment. Some progress has been made during this century. Statistically, the number of women in the 'labour force', i.e. in formal employment, has risen. In many countries legislation has been passed and official agencies have been set up to ensure that discrimination against women in employment does not take place. Awareness of the nature of discrimination against women, and of its importance as an employment question, has become widespread.

But although some progress has been made, there is still a long way to go before women enjoy equal rights and equal opportunities with men in formal employment. This can be seen at a glance from the fact that the annual earnings of women who have jobs average out at around 60% of men's annual earnings. And it is well known that women are poorly represented in the top jobs in almost every walk of life. There are two underlying reasons why women have not made more progress in formal employment. The first is that, because the formal economy is still implicitly regarded as the sphere of men, the work done there (i.e. employment) is organised in ways that suit the needs of men, not women. The second is that, because the informal economy continues to be implicitly regarded as the sphere of women, women's responsibilities there, for home and family life, are greater than men's; and this means that, in general, the degree of commitment that women can make to their work in the formal economy is less than men can make. It adds up to a double burden for many women. Their jobs and the pay that goes with them are, on average, less good than those of men; and they have less leisure than men because of their larger share of responsibility for the informal work at home.

This situation is not peculiar to western capitalist countries. A recent book on *Women, Work and Family in the Soviet Union* makes it clear that:

while Soviet authors routinely decry the double burden which working women continue to bear, and enjoin men to assume a greater share of responsibility for domestic chores, few directly confront the fundamental sources of the problem. The household continues to be viewed as preeminently a female domain, and the family as a female responsibility. The fundamental assumption of Soviet economic and family policy—that women, and women alone, have dual roles – is a continuing barrier to fundamental improvements in women's position.[20]

In poorer countries the position is just as bad, if not worse. The bias in favour of the formal economy, which is a basic cause of the discrimination against which women have to contend, can be even more stark:

> The task of water-carrying is one of the most arduous and indispensable of daily tasks in areas with no piped water. It is almost always the responsibility of women, sometimes assisted by children. Even when a dwelling is located near a water source, drawing water and taking it to the house is a heavy chore. But vast numbers of people live at some distance from a source and the job of lugging containers of water on head or back often takes hours each day. Yet, of 70 developing countries covered in an Organization for Economic Cooperation and Development (OECD) survey, only six included the value of water drawn and carried to the point of use in their definitions of goods and services produced. In one of the six, Kenya, the survey found that 'since women have virtually no employment opportunities in certain pastoral areas of the country, the collection of water in these regions is excluded from economic calculations by government statisticians'. In the same region, however, if a man did the same task in exactly the same way, it would be counted as work.[21]

So, looking to the future, what approaches are there to this whole question of the double burden of women's work, and the double discrimination women now suffer as junior partner in formal employment and senior partner in the informal work of the home?

The first approach, corresponding broadly to Business As Usual, accepts that the present preponderance of the formal economy will and should continue, and regards the present balance of women's employment and household roles as more or less satisfactory. It focuses on incremental changes that will lighten both sides of the burden; further reforms that will continue to improve women's rights and opportunities in employment; and further improvements in services and facilities, public and private, like nursery schools and super-markets, that will make it easier for women to manage the household.

The second approach, which connects in certain respects with the HE view of the future, envisages the continuing exten-sion of formalised work, and its further encroachment into what is left of the informal sphere. The campaign for wages for housework is an example of this approach. Like many other feminist campaigns it aims to secure more equal treatment for women with men in a man's world which is characterised by the dominance of the formal economy and of paid employ-ment over all other kinds of work. André Gorz interprets this campaign for wages for housework from a Marxist point of view as the 'height of alienation', which is reached 'when it becomes impossible to conceive that an activity should have a goal other than its wage, or be grounded upon other than market relations'. He suggests that, following the strict logic of the capitalist market, the women who support this campaign are calling, not just for the right to work as if they were typical men, but also for proletarianisation as an advance over slavery. They are demanding state remuneration as a means by which to have their work recognised as an impersonal service to society as a whole, and not as a personal service owed by them to their husbands and families. As Gorz says, this approach is in conflict with any attempt to achieve a more balanced, freely chosen distribution of tasks on a personal basis between equal male and female partners.[22]

The third approach, corresponding to the SHE view of the future, envisages just such a balanced, freely chosen sharing of work between men and women, perceiving each other as equal partners. It foresees the crucial area for progress in this respect as being the informal economy. We saw in Chapter 2 that a revival of the informal economy will provide the key to a revival of the formal economy and thus of the economy as a whole. Just so, a revival of participation by men in the work of the informal economy will open up more equal opportunities for participation by women in the formal economy and a

more equal balance between men and women in the economy
as a whole. It will represent a feminisation of economic
life.

The Feminisation of Work
Three factors now point towards the coming feminisation of
work. The first is a question of values. The second is the information revolution. And the third is to do with changes already
taking place in the patterns of work.

First, then, the conventional attribution of higher status to
men's work than to women's work is increasingly coming to be
seen as perverse, as the tasks which have typically fallen to
women are coming to be seen as more important than many
of those which have typically fallen to men. Virginia Novarra[23]
gives a good summary of the tasks which women have been
expected to perform as their contribution to keeping society
going. She refers to these as 'the six tasks'. The first is bearing
children. The second is feeding people. The third is clothing
people. The fourth is tending the weak and the sick. The fifth is
bringing up and educating young children. The sixth is being
in charge of the household. Novarra also mentions the role of
emotional shock-absorber and comforter that women are
expected to play for their husbands and children and
friends.

Some of these women's tasks, like bearing children, are not
even regarded as work. But they are all directly concerned with
meeting essential human needs. Life could not go on without
them. By contrast, as Novarra points out, much men's work is
in 'surplus' occupations, in the sense that the physical needs of
the people engaging in them, e.g. for food, clothing and
shelter, have to be met from other people's surplus production. Occupations of this kind include warfare, religion, law
and government, and science, learning and the arts – all of
which have been regarded as masculine occupations. In the
industrial age men's work has become more abstract, impersonal and instrumental than it was in pre-industrial times.
Men have typically shuffled things around in factories, they
have shuffled papers around in offices, they have shuffled
money around in banks, and they have shuffled ideas around
in universities. Women, on the other hand, have been directly
concerned with meeting the needs of people.

As values shift away from the masculine towards the feminine, many typically masculine kinds of work are already beginning to be seen as less useful and more damaging, and the general image of traditiional men's work is becoming less attractive. This will be compounded by the second of the three factors I mentioned, the impact of new technology on the traditional work activities of the macho male. As automation and the microprocessor become more deeply entrenched, the old heavy industries – coal, steel, ship-building, engineering, construction, and so on – will continue to require less work from physically sturdy males. Something like a crisis of masculine identity may have to be surmounted. I have sometimes wondered, as I have been working on this book during the British mineworkers' strike of 1984, whether the battles between the pickets and the police may be symptomatic of a crisis of male identity of that kind. At all events, we seem to be entering a period when deeply disturbing questions are beginning to arise about the value of the work that has been typical of men and about the need for men to do that kind of work in the future.

The third factor is the growing realisation that women's experience of work is likely to have greater value and relevance for many people – including men – in the future.[24] Increasing numbers of people are beginning to feel that the normal pattern of working life in the future will not be modelled on the existing pattern of life-long full-time employment that has been typical for men in industrialised societies, but on the more flexible mixture of part-time employment, family work at home, and voluntary work, mixed in with spells of full-time employment, that has been more typical of many women's working lives in recent decades.

The Valuation of Work

Changes in people's outlook and system of values from time to time over the centuries have prompted discussion of a whole series of essentially technical and philosophical questions about how work and its results are to be valued. The history of economic thinking is shot through with attempts to tackle these questions, ranging from the medieval theory of the just wage and the just price to the late-20th-century conundrum of how to find a sound basis for a national incomes policy.

These questions presented themselves in one way during the middle ages and in another during the industrial age. Now, as we enter the post-industrial age, they are beginning to present themselves in another way again.

Briefly, medieval society assumed that economic relations were governed by a moral law, objective and God-given; and that everything, including work, had its proper value and its just price. To charge more or give less than the just wage or the just price was a sin. Authority, including theological authority, gave guidance on how to decide what was just. In the industrial age the moral and theological approach was replaced by a scientific, humanistic approach. Objectively existing real values and natural prices were assumed to underlie actual economic transactions, and it was assumed to be an aim of economic science to discover what these real values and natural prices were. All value was assumed to be created by human work. And the further assumption was made that value-creating work had to be productive, in the sense of harnessing the physical resources of nature to human use. In the later industrial age the first and the third of these assumptions were modified. The search for real values and natural prices was abandoned, and economists concentrated their attention on how prices, including the price of work (i.e. wages and salaries), actually behaved. It also became accepted that working to provide a service could create value, no less than working to produce tangible goods.

Now, as we move into the post-industrial age, further changes may be expected. The assumption that all value is created by human work seems increasingly questionable, as much traditional work becomes unnecessary and as shortages of natural resources like good land, clean water, and clear air make the value of those things plain. Growing concern is expressed that conventional economic thinking is not sane, or humane, or ecological: it ignores the value of much useful work, especially informal work, that meets human needs; it ignores the value of social justice; and it ignores the value of conserving the planet and its resources. In short, the assumptions of industrial-age economics are now being questioned seriously, and a new approach is beginning to attract support– not authoritarian as in the middle ages, nor supposedly objective in a scientific sense as in the industrial age. This new, more independently personal approach reflects the shift from outer-directed to inner-directed values discussed in the last chapter. It encourages people to rely more on their own sense of values, in contrast to prevailing money values, as a yardstick for assessing the work which they and other people do. It is, obviously, linked with the move towards ownwork.

The Theory of the Just Price

To the medieval mind economic activity was subordinate to morality and the hope of religious salvation. As Tawney put it, 'There is no place in medieval theory for economic activity which is not related to a moral end.' For that reason the appetite for economic gain, no less than the sexual instinct or the propensity to physical violence, was hedged around by moral rules and religious prohibitions.[1]

These rules and prohibitions owed their effectiveness to the fact that medieval society was personal, hierarchical and static, as well as fundamentally religious. People knew personally the people with whom they entered into economic transactions – for whom they carried out work or who carried out work for them, to whom they sold or from whom they bought. 'Much that is now mechanical was then personal, intimate and direct, and there was little room for organisation on a scale too vast for the standards that are applied to individuals.' And people knew what was due to them in their station in life. These things did not change. This social setting reinforced the religious ideas of a just wage and a just price.

It was St. Thomas Aquinas who defined the just price by laying down that the price for which something was sold should correspond with the labour and costs of the producer. This foreshadowed the labour theory of value later developed by John Locke and Adam Smith, and adopted by Karl Marx. As interpreted in the middle ages, it mean that the profits of trade had to be justified by treating them as the wages of the trader, and that it was reprehensible to seek trading gains in excess of a reasonable remuneration. The trader must seek gain, not as an end in itself, but as the wages of his labour. Prices should be such, and no more than such, as would enable each man to have the necessaries of life suitable for his station. Prices should be fixed by public officials in the light of available supplies and the requirements of the producers. Failing that, the individual must fix prices for himself, guided by a consideration of 'what he must charge in order to maintain his position, and nourish himself suitably in it, and by a reasonable estimate of his expenditure and his labour'.

In later centuries there grew up on the medieval theory of the just wage and the just price that whole regulatory superstructure of guilds, corporations and other institutions of the mercantilist state that eventually formed a systemic obstacle to further economic progress. It had to be by-passed and cleared away as part of the great transformation that brought in the industrial age. Just so today there has grown up on the theoretical foundations of industrial-age economics the institutional superstructure of business, finance, trade unions, professions and government that now constitutes a systemic obstacle to further economic development and social progress. It, in its turn, will have to be by-passed and cleared away as part of the great transformation that will bring in the post-industrial age. But that is to jump ahead.

The Labour Theory of Value

John Locke developed Aquinas' theory of the just price into the labour theory of value, according to which it is work that creates value by harnessing the resources of nature to human use. 'It is labour indeed that puts the difference of value on everything. . . . If we will rightly estimate things as they come to our use and cast up the several expenses about them – what in them is purely owing to Nature and what to labour – we shall find that in most of them ninety-nine hundredths are wholly to be put on the account of labour.' Locke regarded labour as the basis of property too. Whatever a man 'removes out of the state that Nature hath provided and left it in, he hath mixed his labour with it . . . and thereby makes it his property'. 'Though the water running in the fountain be everyone's, yet who can doubt the water in the pitcher is his only who drew it out? His labour hath taken it out of the hand of Nature where it was common, and belonged equally to all her children, and hath thereby appropriated it to himself.'[2]

Adam Smith agreed with Locke in giving pride of place to work as the source of value. The introduction to *The Wealth of Nations*[3] begins with the following words: 'The annual labour of every nation is the fund which originally supplies it with all the necessaries and conveniences of life which it annually consumes, and which consists always either in the immediate produce of that labour, or in what is purchased with that produce from other nations.' Smith then goes on to discuss the causes of improvement in the productive powers of labour, and Book One, Chapter One, contains his famous discussion on specialisation and division of labour as the source of increasing wealth and economic growth. As the following paragraphs show, Adam Smith went to great pains to argue that wealth and value are based on work, and that wealth – as well as being ultimately derived from work – is to be measured by the amount of other people's work it enables its possessor to command.

> Every man is rich or poor according to the degree in which he can afford to enjoy the necessaries, conveniences, and amusements of human life. But after the division of labour has once thoroughly taken place, it is but a very small part of these with which a man's own labour can supply him. The far greater part of them he must derive from the labour of other people, and he must be rich or poor according to the quantity of that labour which he can command, or which he can afford to purchase. The value of any commodity, therefore, to the person who possesses it, and who means not to use or consume it

himself, but to exchange it for other commodities, is equal to the quantity of labour which it enables him to purchase or command. Labour, therefore, is the real measure of the exchangeable value of all commodities.

The real price of everything, what everything really costs to the man who wants to acquire it, is the toil and trouble of acquiring it. What everything is really worth to the man who has acquired it, and who wants to dispose of it or exchange it for something else, is the toil and trouble which it can save to himself, and which it can impose upon other people. What is bought with money or with goods is purchased by labour as much as what we acquire by the toil of our own body. That money or those goods indeed save us this toil. They contain the value of a certain quantity of labour which we exchange for what is supposed at the time to contain the value of an equal quantity. Labour was the first price, the original purchase-money that was paid for all things. It was not by gold or by silver, but by labour, that all the wealth of the world was originally purchased; and its value, to those who possess it, and who want to exchange it for some new productions, is precisely equal to the quantity of labour which it can enable them to purchase or command.

Wealth, as Mr Hobbes says, is power. But the person who either acquires, or succeeds to a great fortune, does not necessarily acquire or succeed to any political power, either civil or military. His fortune may, perhaps, afford him the means of acquiring both, but the mere possession of that fortune does not necessarily convey to him either. The power which that possession immediately and directly conveys to him, is the power of purchasing; a certain command over all the labour, or over all the produce of labour, which is then in the market. His fortune is greater or less, precisely in proportion to the extent of this power; or to the quantity either of other men's labour, or, what is the same thing, of the produce of other men's labour, which it enables him to purchase or command. The exchangeable value of everything must always be precisely equal to the extent of this power which it conveys to its owner.

But though labour be the real measure of the exchangeable value of all commodities, it is not that by which their value is commonly estimated. It is often difficult to ascertain the proportion between two different quantities of labour. The time spent in two different sorts of work will not always alone determine this proportion. The different degrees of hardship endured, and of ingenuity exercised, must likewise be taken into account. There may be more labour in an hour's hard work than in two hours' easy business; or in an hour's application to a trade which it cost ten years' labour to learn, than in a month's industry at an ordinary and obvious employment. But it is not easy to find any accurate measure either of hardship or ingenuity. In exchanging, indeed, the different productions of different sorts of labour for one another, some allowance is commonly made for both. It is adjusted, however, not by any accurate measure, but by the higgling and bargaining of the market, according to that sort of rough equality which, though not exact, is sufficient for carrying on the business of common life.

In spite of this lack of precision, Smith insisted that labour, 'never varying in its own value, is alone the ultimate and real standard by which the value of all commodities can at all times and places be estimated and compared. It is their real price; money is their nominal price only'.

For Marx, as for Locke and Smith, the one and only source of value was productive labour used to harness material resources to satisfy human needs. He regarded uncultivated land, for example, as 'not being a value' because no human labour has been incorporated in it. But, whereas Smith hoped the labour theory of value would provide a firm basis for measuring wealth, including the wealth of the nation and the national product, Marx developed it to explain the nature of exploitation in a capitalist society.[4]

In a capitalist society, Marx argued, the wage-earner has to sell his labour-power (not his labour, as such), because he has nothing else to sell. According to the labour theory of value, the value of labour-power is, like the value of all commodities, determined by the labour needed to produce it. The production of labour-power involves keeping the worker fit for work and enabling him to reproduce a new generation of workers. Thus the value of the labour-power which the employee sells to his employer is equal to the cost of the employee's subsistence. Exploitation arises because, having purchased the wage-earner's labour-power for the cost of his subsistence, the employer is able to use the wage-earner's labour to create greater values than that subsistence cost. If, in half a day, the worker's labour can produce products of a value equivalent to his subsistence cost, the other half-day's unrequited labour creates surplus value for the owner of the means of production for whom the worker is working.

The labour theory of value, as developed by Smith and Marx, reflected the outlook of the early industrial age in several respects.

First, it assumed that a product or commodity had a real value, which might differ from the actual price obtained or given for it. The actual price could be affected by local or temporary conditions in the market, or by fluctuations in the value of money. But, other things being equal, there would be a tendency for actual prices to approximate to real values. This economic idea of real value (or natural price, as it was sometimes called) was of a piece with the political ideas of natural laws and natural rights behind the American and French Revolutions. Both were consonant with the prevailing model of science. The idea that real values lay beneath the surface phenomena of market prices, and that these real values could be calculated (in terms of the labour used to create them), paralleled the teaching of Newtonian science that beneath the surface phenomena of the natural world there lay real matter in the form of atoms whose properties and behaviour could, at least in principle, be observed and measured. However, Smith and Marx failed to find a way to measure the real value of products as distinct from their price, because they could not establish an objective measure of labour input which could serve as a basis for calculating real values. The later neoclassical economists gave up both the search for real values and the labour theory of value, and concentrated on studying prices – a good example of the prevalent industrial-age tendency for attention to migrate to that half of the Cartesian dualism that could be quantitatively measured.

Second, the labour theory of value assumed that valuable or productive work was work that harnessed *material* resources and produced *material* objects to satisfy human needs. Even when John Stuart Mill argued later that the work involved in the training of workers might be regarded as productive, he felt it necessary to add: 'provided that an increase of material products is its ultimate consequence'.[5] This assumption had its roots in the religious doctrine of earlier times, which taught that God had given man dominion over nature. The more recent scientific tradition, articulated by Francis Bacon in the early 17th century, took this further and urged man to extend his mastery over the forces of nature by means of scientific discoveries and inventions. The tremendous breakthroughs of the early industrial age in manufacturing and transport confirmed the success of this approach. Progress was now seen to be based on the development of human capacity to harness the material world to human use. No wonder Marx responded to Hegel's perception of labour – man's physical commerce with nature – as the process by which humanity externalises itself and develops its own essence, and came to see man's work upon nature as the condition of all spiritual human activity, by which man creates himself as well as nature. Contemporary Catholic thinking still endorses this outer-directed view of human development.

> Man has to subdue the earth and dominate it, because as the image of God he is a person, that is to say a subjective being capable of acting in a planned and rational way, capable of deciding about himself, and with a tendency to self-realisation. . . . Understood as a process whereby man and the human race subdue the earth, work corresponds to this basic biblical concept only when throughout the process man manifests himself and confirms himself as the one who dominates.[6]

The later neo-classical economists abandoned the idea that only material production creates value. They accepted that the provision of services creates value too. Nonetheless, the early emphasis on work as physical production supported a perception of wealth as consisting of material things which has lasted until today. In the 18th and 19th centuries this also linked with the primacy given to property in the political sphere.

Third, the labour theory of value attached no value to unworked natural resources, such as water or air or uncultivated land. Land did, of course, have a price. In Britain the enclosures of common land in the 17th and 18th centuries meant that most land was privately owned. Like work and money, land had become a commodity that could be bought and sold. But Smith and Marx could still argue that the real value of land stemmed from the work that had previously been put into it. In their day natural resources seemed inexhaustible, and could be treated as if they would continue to be freely available for ever. Only now, toward the end of the 20th century, are we beginning to question this.

Fourth, the labour theory of value assumed the primacy of work in the formal economy which produces goods and services for exchange, over work in the informal economy which produces goods and services for direct use by the producers themselves or by their family, friends and neighbours. It is true that, in discussing the values created by work, Smith explicitly distinguished between use-value and exchange-value: 'The word "value", it is to be observed, has two different meanings, and sometimes expresses the utility of some particular object, and sometimes the power of purchasing other goods which the possession of that object conveys. The one may be called "value in use"; the other, "value in exchange".' But Smith set the pattern for all economists after him, including Marx, by limiting himself to investigating 'the principles which regulate the exchangeable value of commodities'. He was not interested in the workings of the informal economy where production is for direct use, but only in the workings of the formal economy in which goods and services are produced for exchange. He assumed that 'after the division of labour has once thoroughly taken place' we must largely depend on the formal economy for the necessities of life. This assumption still dominates discussion of economic matters today, and it is only in the last few years that it has begun to be seriously questioned.

Finally, a feature of the labour theory of value stressed by Adam Smith in the passage quoted earlier was the idea that wealth was to be measured by the amount of other people's work it enabled the possessor to purchase or command. To be wealthy was to be able to have a lot of other people working for you, indirectly if not directly. This interpretation of wealth fitted the dawning age of employment no less than it had the ages of serfdom and slavery that were past. It has certainly not yet been abandoned. But it has lost some of its pertinence in the last 200 years, and it is likely to be questioned more positively as the post-industrial revolution proceeds. We shall return to this point at the end of this chapter.

The Neo-Classical Economists

The neo-classical economists, as I have said, abandoned the

search for real values and natural prices. Instead, they concentrated on the study of market prices. In a narrow sense this cleared the decks. Economists were now able to study how actual, observable economic transactions took place and how actual, observable prices behaved, without the distraction of wondering what unobservable real values and natural prices were lurking beneath them. (In fact, many economists decided to study how prices *would* behave in a non-existent, mathematically rational world. But that is another matter.)

From a broader point of view, however, it was unfortunate that economists dropped their concern with values. This automatically restricted their sphere of interest to the formal economy (in which prices operated), to paid work, and to 'demand' that was backed by money. It confirmed the exclusion from economics, not only of questions about the possible need to conserve unworked natural resources, but also of questions about the unpaid work of the informal economy by which people provide goods and services – utilities, use-values, or satisfactions – directly to themselves and one another. It restricted economic activities to two categories only. The first, production, was assumed to be wealth-creating; the second, consumption, was assumed to be wealth-consuming. It attributed no economic significance to production for use (as opposed to production for exchange) or to activities carried out for their own sake. Strictly speaking, it also excluded from economics all needs and wants (such as those of poor people) not sufficiently backed with money to generate effective demand for the goods and services required to meet them. This last exclusion was later rectified, in part, by the development of public sector economics and the use of government taxation, borrowing and spending to create new patterns of effective demand (and provide public services) to meet needs which an uncorrected market economy would have ignored. Nonetheless, by disclaiming any interest in non-monetary values, the neo-classical economists disqualified themselves – and their successors to this day – from discussing the widening range of needs which cannot be satisfied by monetary purchases or by services provided at public expense. These include personal needs, e.g. for responsibility and self-confidence; social needs, e.g. for mutual respect and mutual co-operation; and environmental needs, e.g. for the conservation of natural resources.

However, one useful consequence of the abandonment by the neo-classical economists of the idea of real value and their concentration on money prices was that they no longer attributed value to material products only. The criterion of whether something had value now became whether people would buy it. If there was a demand for a service, and people would pay for it, then it had value; and the work that went into providing it could be regarded as productive. In economic terms, it was the production of utilities or satisfactions that mattered, not the production of material objects as such. As Alfred Marshall put it, writing in 1890, 'Man cannot create material things, he really only produces utilities . . . It is sometimes said that traders do not produce: that while the cabinet-maker produces furniture, the furniture dealer merely sells what is already produced. But there is no scientific foundation for this distinction. They both produce utilities, and neither of them can do more.'[7]

The classical distinction between productive and un-productive labour, as labour which produces material pro-ducts and labour which does not, thus evaporated. 'We may define labour', Marshall said, 'as any exertion of mind or body undergone partly or wholly with a view to some good other than the pleasure derived directly from the work. And if we had to make a fresh start, it would be best to regard all labour as productive, except that which failed to promote the aim towards which it was directed, and so produced no utility.'

This development in neo-classical economics prefigured the great growth of service trades and industries in the 20th century. By 1950 or thereabouts service-led economies had emerged in industrialised countries like the United States and Britain – service-led in the sense that services became the main growth area for employment and the largest sector of economic activity. Today most of those who foresee a return to economic growth and full employment rely on a further expansion of the service industries – including what they call the information, knowledge and leisure industries – to achieve it. Indeed they believe that most new wealth will now be created by the production and sale of information, knowledge and leisure, and they attach a high value to work done in these spheres.

The Supremacy of Quantitative Values

The abandonment by the neo-classical economists of the idea of real value and their concentration on money prices can be seen as a final step in the shift from qualitative values to quantitative values that distinguished the outlook of the industrial age from the outlook of the middle ages.

The supremacy of quantitative values is reflected in Lord Kelvin's famous dictum that 'when you can measure what you are speaking of and express it in numbers, you know that on which you are discoursing, but when you cannot measure it and express it in numbers, your knowledge is of a very meagre and unsatisfactory kind'. Applied to economic and social life this means: when you can measure the value of what you do for other people and they do for you (i.e. work), the value of what you possess (i.e. wealth), the value of what you receive (i.e. revenues or income), the value of what you give out (i.e. costs or expenditure), and the difference in value between revenues and costs (i.e. profit/loss), you know where you are and can work out what you ought to do; but when you cannot measure these things your life will be in a muddle.

Our calculus for measuring economic and social values is, of course, money; and the growing role of money in our lives, and the growing role of financial institutions in society, are direct reflections of our increasing concern for quantitative values. Moreover, the growing importance of money is directly linked to the central feature of the development of work during the industrial age, i.e. the shift from unpaid work done by people for themselves and one another, to paid work in the form of jobs organised by employers. This is now coming to be described as a shift from informal work to formal work, or from work in the informal economy to work in the formal economy.

This concept of a dual economy, meaning that the economy should be regarded as divided into two spheres, formal and informal, is already playing a significant part in economic discussion, and will almost certainly become more important in the next few years.

The formal and informal sectors of the economy are to be seen as two different spheres of activity, two different aspects of every-day life. Everyone in an industrialised society is involved in both of these spheres of activity to a greater or lesser extent. The balance between formal and informal (e.g. the division of time spent in the one sphere and in the other) is different for different people, but everyone takes part to some extent in both. Everyone spends some time on activities that involve earning or spending, and everyone spends some time on activities that do not.

In practice, it may be difficult to draw a hard and fast line between formal and informal activity. This is particularly true of neighbourly or family activities which are accompanied by unrecorded cash payments – for example, for casual work done by, say, window cleaners or jobbing gardeners. Sometimes this blurring of the boundary between formal and informal activity results in what is called the black economy – referring to activities which should be declared as formal, so that they can be taxed or otherwise regulated, but are not declared and are thus illegitimate. But although the boundary between the informal and the formal economy is often blurred, the informal economy is best understood as consisting of the whole range of perfectly legitimate household and neighbourhood activities which are carried out on a person-to-person basis and are taken for granted as being a part of everyone's life.

As the emphasis shifted during the industrial age from informal to formal activity, it came to be assumed that the formal economy was the only part of the economy that mattered. In late industrial societies economists have ignored the contribution of informal economic activities to the wellbeing of people and of society as a whole. They have contented themselves with studying the part of the economy in which activity could be counted – i.e. in which figures could be attached to the amounts of money earned and spent, to the number of jobs provided by employers, to the quantities of goods produced, and so on. Politicians likewise have concentrated on debating how the formal economy can be improved – how to create measurable economic growth and to raise employment levels, whether to cut taxes or raise government borrowing, and so on. They too have ignored the role of the informal economy in the lives of people and society. They have never thought it worth while to discuss what balance we should aim for between formal and informal activity or, for example, whether the formal economy now plays too large a part in most people's lives.

Thus the orthodoxy of the industrial age has been that the formal economy is the only real economy, and that respectable thought and action on economic and·social questions should concentrate only on those activities that have a money tag attached. It has come to be assumed that the only real work is the work which is done in the formal economy – in other words, that paid employment is the only really valid form of work.

The Failure of Quantitative Evaluation
What value should we place on different kinds of work? How much should workers in different fields be paid?

The problem of the just wage returned with a vengeance in late industrial society under the guise of 'incomes policy'. In practice, of course, no government has really tried to introduce an incomes policy with the primary purpose of matching levels of pay fairly with the value of the work done. Some recent governments have even claimed that, although their decisions affect people's income and pay levels, they do not have an incomes policy at all. The primary aim has always been to contain inflation, by keeping pay rises down.

An incomes policy has usually involved introducing a norm – a certain percentage figure which has been intended to govern the average rise in pay levels over a stated period of time. Then – and this is where the process of relative evaluation comes in – exceptional groups of workers have been permitted higher pay rises on specific grounds. For example, in Britain in 1965–70 exceptions were based on: increasing productivity; the need to attract workers to areas of shortage; the need to raise low pay to a level that would maintain a decent standard of living; and the need to bring the pay level into line with what was paid for comparable work elsewhere.

Aubrey Jones, who was chairman of the National Board for Prices and Incomes in Britain at that time, noted that some countries – for example, Holland and certain socialist countries – had tried to establish national job evaluation schemes which would grade jobs throughout the country on a single scale.[8] But, while a job evaluation scheme can help to create a sense of fairness within the comparatively narrow context of a particular organisation, a comprehensive national job evaluation scheme could never be made to work. This is not just because of the complexity of reconciling the conflicting claims of efficiency and fairness on a national scale – including the need that pay should reflect the changing demand for work of different kinds, encourage and recognise productivity, and be comparable with that of other groups of comparable workers. It is also because the remoteness and complexity of a job evaluation scheme on this scale would offer an irresistible challenge to everyone to find ways of getting exceptions made to it in their own favour.

It is not surprising that an incomes policy has never been successful for anything longer than a short emergency period. After all, a propensity to maximise value is an inevitable part of any situation in which quantitative, as opposed to qualitative, values take pride of place. In such a situation people are bound to try to maximise their income, especially when they see those richer and more powerful than themselves doing that all the time. The failure of the incomes policy is symptomatic of the problems that arise once too much emphasis is placed on quantifying the value of work. There are several possible approaches to these problems.

The first is directed to the money system itself. The argument is that, money being the calculus we use to measure value, it is vital that the money system should operate fairly and objectively. Money values should reflect the actual values and preferences that people have; for example, people's pay should reflect the value of the work they do. As things are, however, everyone knows that the money system does not work this way. Some people get highly paid for work of little value, while others get paid much less for work of much greater value. The people who run the money system – bankers, stockbrokers, and so on – do not run it professionally, with the aim that it should operate fairly and efficiently in the interests of society as a whole. They operate it in such a way as to cream off above-average incomes and capital gains for themselves and their clients. In this sense, the present money system is fundamentally corrupt, although the great majority of the people concerned are not personally corrupt or fraudulent in a technical, legal sense. The conclusion of this argument is that reforms in the money system will help to solve some of the problems that now bedevil attempts to quantify the value of work. We shall return to the question of money in Chapter 8.

A second approach is directed to the concepts of macro-economics, and in particular to the concept of economic growth based on measurement of Gross National Product (GNP). The argument is that economic growth, as calculated by economists today, is not a measure of increasing wellbeing or of increasing value in anything other than in a purely artificial sense. On the one hand, it fails to record wellbeing and value created by informal economic activity; so that, for example, if increasing numbers of people grow more of their food for themselves and buy less of it from the shops, the statistics will record a decline in the value of economic activity. On the other hand, it includes as gains the monetary value of many activities that should properly be regarded as costs; so that, for example, if increasing numbers of accidents and misfortunes call forth an increased level of rescue, repair and medical activity – which might properly be regarded as a cost rather than a benefit – the statistics will record an increase in the value of economic activity and therefore of wellbeing. This misleading conceptual framework tends to distort the values given to different kinds of work throughout the economy. Not only is formal work in general valued more highly than infor-mal; but, to take a specific example of two kinds of formal work, the remedial work of curative medicine is valued more highly than the health-creating work which would make the curative work unnecessary. The conclusion is that new indicators of economic performance and social wellbeing must be developed in place of the statistical concepts we use today.

The third and most fundamental approach is based on the need to create a new balance between quantitative and qualitative evaluation. The argument is that, whatever reforms are made in the money system and in the statistical basis for measuring the value of work done, these external ways of measuring value quantitatively can never be more than pseudo-objective. They will always be to some extent arbitrary and distorted. There is no objective way of reflecting accurately the system of values prevailing in a particular society at a particular time, as is shown by the failure of earlier medieval and Smithian/Marxian attempts to define a just wage and an objectively valued unit of labour input. And, even if there were, such a method of valuation could not accommodate either the unconventional values of minority groups and individuals, or the changes that take place in a whole society's system of values over the years. A free society of intelligent men and women must recognise that people's own sense of values will sometimes be at variance with the externalised systems of values reflected in the money system and the prevailing conceptual basis of economic and social theory and statistics. It should encourage them to follow their own inner knowledge in this respect, except when they would be harming others when doing so.

Pointers for the Future
Reform of the money system and changes in the conceptual basis of economic thinking are, then, two types of change which will be needed as we try to adapt to a new future for work, and to develop new ways of evaluating it. We shall return to both in subsequent chapters. But even more important will be for increasing numbers of people to develop a clearer sense of what we really value, and to create conditions in which more and more of us can exercise this sense of value both in decisions about our own work, and in our assessments of other people's.

We no longer believe in the idea of a God-given just wage. We no longer believe that the products and services which people work to provide have objectively quantifiable *real* values, distinct from actual costs and prices. We no longer believe, however, that we can simply rely on the system of costs and prices that actually exist, to define our values for us. We make a distinction between value and price, and we regret that economics has lost sight of it. We know what Oscar Wilde meant when he said that a cynic is someone who knows the price of everything and the value of nothing. We know that, as things are, many people are paid more highly for doing work of less value, while many others are paid less well for doing more valuable work. We regret that, as things are, a huge amount of time and energy is wasted in argument and dispute about levels of pay.

In an age, such as the post-industrial age will be, in which the development of ourselves through our own experiences and activities is seen as a primary purpose in life, it is likely that relatively less store will be placed on *having* than on *being*. It will become less valuable to have other people working for us, than to be able to undertake important activities and life-experiences for ourselves. It will come to be experienced as less valuable to consume the planet's resources unnecessarily, than to act in ways that conserve them. Above all, it will come to be seen as desirable to work in personal and local contexts. A more direct meeting of real needs than most formal work achieves today will enable people to make and share with one another direct, intuitive, qualitative valuations of the work they do.

PART 3

THE END OF THE EMPLOYMENT EMPIRE

The power structures of late industrial society have been based on the fact that employment has been the dominant form of work. Among these structures of power, three, in addition to employers in general, have been pre-eminent: the organised labour movement; the financial system; and the system of representative politics and bureaucratic government. During the industrial age these have developed as the most powerful branches of an ever more dominating empire on which people have become increasingly dependent. The transition from the industrial to the post-industrial age, and from employment to ownwork, will involve a reversal of that industrial-age trend.

It is, in fact, helpful to see the transition from employment to ownwork as the end of an empire – the breakdown of the employment empire and the liberation of its subjects from their present dependence on it. The process of transition will then have two different aspects, depending on where you stand. First, it will involve managing the breakdown of the old empire, in other words its decolonisation. Second, it will involve liberating yourself – and helping to liberate other people – from being dependent on it. This way of understanding the nature of the transition will underlie our discussion of its practicalities in Part 4.

Meanwhile, in Part 3, we explore the implications of the transition to ownwork for organised labour, for the financial system, and for politics and government. How will it be likely to affect them? And what part may they be able and required to play in bringing it about?

8

Labour

The working class and the organised labour movement were created by the industrial revolution. They have been pheno-mena of the employment age. Their early history is a testa-ment to the courage of working-class leaders, to the endurance of working-class people, to the vision they continued to nurture of creating a better society, and to the working-class culture they founded on collective solidarity and mutual aid. You can-not read about it – in books like E. P. Thompson's *The Making of the English Working Class* – without being deeply moved.

By the early-20th century the organised labour movement had so developed in strength that it had become established as a power in the land. In Britain in the 1920s its links with the Labour Party brought it into the counsels of government, and in the second half of the 20th century it has been treated in most industrialised countries as one of the major partners in economic life, along with employers and government. By the 1960s the trade union movement in Britain was already com-ing under criticism for exercising unaccountable power, and attempts began to be made to limit by changes in the law the damage which could be caused by unnecessary and irrespons-ible industrial action in the form of strikes. Now, in the 1980s, as the end of the employment age comes nearer, a question mark hangs over the whole future of the working class and the organised labour movement.

If a key feature of the bourgeois work ethic in the early days was individual self-help, a key feature of the working-class ethic in the early days was collective mutual aid. In principle, a post-industrial work order, characterised by ownwork in place of employment, will need to be based on a combination of self-help and mutual aid in a new ethic of co-operative self-reliance. In Chapter 5 we suggested that some aspects of the Puritan work ethic might contribute directly to this. What strands in working-class culture, as it has now developed, could be woven into the fabric of the new work ethic? How far is the trade union movement likely to contribute to the development of ownwork? And, conversely, how far is it likely to regard the prospect of ownwork as a threat to its own continuing existence and survival?

Defensive Posture

There is a great difficulty here, which must be faced at the start. This is the essential defensiveness of the working-class outlook. It derives from the dominant working-class experience of being forced to respond to changes imposed by others, and compelled to act within a structure of society not created by themselves. This habit of perception and response, though entirely understandable and in no way to be blamed, could nonetheless be a dangerous weakness at a time when a new order of society and a new work order are coming into existence. It could easily channel energy into resisting inevitable change, instead of helping to shape the future that is to be. The response of the organised labour movement to today's unemployment crisis can be interpreted this way.

The fact, of course, is that the history of the last 200 years is studded with attempts by working people to resist having changes forced upon them that were damaging and unfair. The very origin of the working class was in the expropriation of common rights to land, the transformation of independent craftsmen and tradespeople into dependent wage-workers, and the gross exploitation in mines and factories of men, women and children – many of whom could see before their eyes in the space of a few years that their poorly paid labour had made their masters rich.

Consciousness of belonging to the working class grew out of the shared experience of those who suffered injustice at the hands of others who felt no sense of humanity or social obligation towards them. E.P. Thompson[1] refers to a journeyman cotton spinner of 1818 who based the sense of grievance of working people on:

> the rise of a master-class without traditional authority or obligations; the growing distance between master and man; the transparency of the exploitation at the source of their new

wealth and power; the loss of status and above all of independence for the worker, and his reduction to total dependence on the master's means of production; the partiality of the law; the disruption of the family economy; the discipline, monotony, hours and conditions of work; loss of leisure and amenities; the reduction of man to the status of an instrument.

In social, economic, political and cultural terms, the changes of the early industrial age impinged on most working people as changes for the worse – whatever economists' calculations may show about the standard of living, and in spite of the fact that some men and women experienced these changes as a liberation from the rural hardships and social immobility of earlier times.

The best-known example of working-class resistance to change was the Luddite movement of the early 19th century. The Luddites were resisting not only the introduction of particular types of new machines, but also the development of the factory system and the degradation that it meant for the lives of working people. They were resisting the destruction of community, and the replacement of what was left of the old social fabric based on reciprocal rights and duties by the harsh impersonal imperatives of laisser faire.

E.P. Thompson sees Luddism as a moment of transitional conflict. On the one hand the Luddites were some of the last guildsmen, looking back to old customs and the paternalist legislation of the past. On the other hand, he says, many of their demands – for example, for a minimum wage, arbitration, the right to have trade unions – pointed forward to the more democratic industrial society of the 20th century, in which economic growth and the pursuit of profit would be regulated by social constraints. That no doubt looks true from a historical point of view, as we look back on the Luddites with the benefit of hindsight 170 years later. But from their point of view at that time, the Luddites were surely pitting their energies *against* the changes then being imposed. They were not concerned to create a new society based on a positive vision of a future different from the present and the past, with which they were familiar.

This oppositional, defensive stance of resistance to change has remained an important aspect of working-class attitudes and Marxist thinking right to the present day. And with good reason. As writers like Harry Braverman[2] and Mike Cooley[3] convincingly show, the original expropriation of the capacity of working people to control their own work, by the enclosure of land and the coming of the factory system, has been continued in management practices and management innovations ever since. The object of these has always been to give managements greater control over the work ·of their employees.

The outstanding example has been Taylorism, the scientific approach to the management of other people's work which was developed by Frederick Taylor in the United States in the 1880s and the 1890s. Before Taylor, managements had introduced various ways of controlling their workers: having them work in the factory rather than at home; dictating the length of their working day; supervising them, setting production minimums and making other rules that discouraged slacking; and so on. But, as Braverman says, 'Taylor raised the concept of control to an entirely new plane when he asserted as an absolute necessity for adequate management the dictation to the worker of the precise manner in which work is to be performed.'

In the late 20th century Taylor's approach has been taken to extraordinary lengths. As Mike Cooley puts it, 'So totally does the employer seek to subordinate the worker to production, that he asserts that the worker's every minute and every movement "belong" to him, the employer . . . The grotesque precision with which this is done to workers can be seen from . . . particulars of the . . . 32.4 minute rest allowance deal for body press workers on the Allegro ear:

Trips to the lavatory	1.62 minutes
For fatigue	1.3 minutes
Sitting down after standing too long	65 seconds
For monotony	32 seconds

and so the grotesque litany goes on.'

Throughout the industrial age, what Braverman calls the step-by-step creation of a labour force in place of self-directed human labour was resisted at every step by those on whom it was imposed. But, increasingly, as the strength of organised labour grew, each step became the subject of negotiation between employer and employees, with the latter eventually agreeing to sell some loss of their previous control over the work process, in return for an increased wage. Resistance to change shaded into negotiation about the terms on which change would be accepted.

So workers no longer questioned that work should take the form of employment. Antagonism remained between employee and employer, and many employees got little or no satisfaction from employment. But the memory and the vision faded of ownwork as a better way to work. And now, as the age of employment comes towards an end, resistance to change understandably centres on the threatened loss of jobs. Ivan Illich need not be surprised that the rioting cottagers of the early industrial years, defending their right to work for their own subsistence and protesting against being reduced to the status of wage-workers, are now replaced by the striking and picketing employees of the late industrial years, defending their right to wage-work and protesting at the loss of jobs.[4]

The Lucas Initiative
How deeply this defensive stance is rooted in a sense of dependency on the status quo, and of the need to preserve it, is illustrated by the outcome of one of the most imaginative initiatives taken in recent years by organised employees. This was the workers' corporate plan drawn up in the 1970s under the auspices of the Lucas Aerospace Shopstewards Combine Committee. The plan formed the basis for the campaign for the right to work on socially useful products. The Lucas workers proposed a new range of socially useful products which they and their company could produce, including a 'hobcart' for children with spina bifida, a life-support system, energy-conserving products, a hybrid power pack, all-purpose power generation equipment for third world countries, a road/rail vehicle, kidney machines, and telechiric devices. In Mike Cooley's words, they showed that they were able to propose 'a whole series of new methods of production where workers by hand and brain can really contribute to the design and development of products, and where they can

work in a non-alienated manner in a labour process which enhances human beings rather than diminishes them'.

The Lucas initiative attracted widespread international attention. It was perceived as an exciting pointer to a future in which production would be geared to social uses, and workers would have much more opportunity to work on products which they regarded as valuable, in ways which were more under their own control.

In spite of first appearances, however, the Lucas workers' initiative turned out to be essentially defensive. In evaluating what it achieved, Hilary Wainwright and Dave Elliott stress that it had its origin in the fight to save jobs.[5] Their verdict is that the 'plan for socially useful production enabled the Lucas workers to defend the status quo on jobs, until an increase in orders for military aerospace systems reduced the immediate pressure for redundancies'. That was important for the Lucas workers. But it was not a positive outcome to a campaign to stop working in armaments production and convert to making socially useful products.

In assessing the extent to which that more far-reaching aim of the Lucas workers was achieved, Wainwright and Elliott conclude that the tangible achievement was small. 'In summary . . . Lucas as a company has developed some of the ideas in the corporate plan in some form or another, in the main outside the Aerospace division. But, with the exception of the electric vehicles, these and its other diversification efforts have not been backed with substantial resources – and most have now been wound up.' The problem, as Wainwright and Elliott – and the Lucas workers themselves – saw it, was the capitalist stance of Lucas. The crucial reason why the company never seriously considered the workers' corporate plan was that 'for top management, the right to manage does not simply mean the freedom to get on with the technical tasks of management without interference. It is the right to manage in the interest of the shareholders'.

I once asked one of the leading members of the Lucas Aerospace Shopstewards Combine Committee whether those who initiated the Lucas workers' corporate plan had ever considered leaving the company and setting up a workers' co-operative to produce some of the socially useful products that the plan had proposed. He told me that this was ruled out.

The original aim behind the corporate plan had been to safeguard Lucas workers' jobs. If the leaders of the initiative had left the company to set up a co-operative, they would have left their fellow workers in the lurch. Thus the Lucas workers felt precluded from exercising any direct autonomous power of decision over their own work, and from taking effective steps to create for themselves the right which they sought to work on socially useful products, if necessary by leaving their capitalist employer, Lucas. Their only course of action, as they and their supporters saw it, was an indirect one. They should work for a new socialist politics in the hope of one day getting a sympathetic socialist government elected that would give them the right they sought.

The sense of dependency underlying their solidarity is suggested by the following statement by Ernie Scarbrow, the Secretary of the Combine Committee: 'It is outrageous that our members in Lucas Aerospace are being made redundant when the state has to find them £40 a week to do nothing except suffer the degradation of the dole queue. In fact the £40 a week amounts to about £70 a week when the cost of administration is taken into account. Our workers *should be given* this money and *allowed* to produce socially useful products such as the kidney machines' (my italics).[6]

This sense of dependency has been a natural part of the outlook of the labour movement and the working class. It is amply justified by the facts of practical life and by the experience of working people over the last 200 years. The same cannot be said for the equivalent sense of dependency when it is expressed by more privileged people. Take, for example, the people in charge of a firm of high-powered research consultants, who 'were longing to prove themselves by solving major social problems; but they were hardly ever *given* anything but industrial and business questions' (my italics). I wonder whether, in reporting this, Robert Jungk[7] believed that these people really could solve major social problems, or whether he saw them – as I do – as helpless, spoilt, overgrown boys complaining that the grown-ups wouldn't allow them to play more glamorous games with their sophisticated toys.

The reason why the element of dependency and the lack of autonomy in the outlook of organised labour is so significant, is because it could prove to be a damaging source of vulnerability in the transition to a new work order. In a situation of failed dependency such as we are living in today, it becomes increasingly fruitless to make claims on institutions which are becoming increasingly incapable of meeting them. The energy spent on demanding that other people should organise socially useful work – or, for that matter, almost anything else – for us is likely to be more effectively spent organising it for ourselves.

Work Rights and Responsibilities
The right to work on socially useful products is one among many rights that have been claimed for employees. In fact in the 200 years since most people lost the right of access to land and the other means of production with which they had supported their work, and thus became dependent on employers to provide them with work, there has been notable progress in people's rights as regards employment. The French Declaration of the Rights of Man in 1789 did not even mention rights at work or the right to work. Compare that with the United Nations Universal Declaration of Human Rights in 1948, Article 23 of which declared:

(1) Everyone has the right to work, to free choice of employment, to just and favourable conditions of work and to protection against unemployment.
(2) Everyone, without any discrimination, has the right to equal pay for equal work.
(3) Everyone who works has the right to just and favourable remuneration ensuring for himself and his family an existence worthy of human dignity, and supplemented, if necessary, by other means of social protection.
(4) Everyone has the right to form and to join trade unions for the protection of his interests.

The right to a job; the rights of employees to decent conditions of work, to organise in trade unions, and to negotiate terms and conditions with their employer; equal employment rights, if not positive discrimination, for disadvantaged sections of society – including women, racial and religious minorities, and handicapped people; the right to be compensated for being unfairly sacked; the growth of trade union strength; the development of industrial relations procedures; new laws to regulate employment; the efforts of progressive employers to improve the 'quality of working life' – all these are new and important. They have helped to reduce injustice and improve conditions of work for many people.

But there is another side to the coin.

The assumption underlying these developments has been that work takes place in the context of employment; most people cannot aspire to work on their own account. Only a privileged few can claim the right to be responsible for directing their energies to purposes they themselves regard as valuable; for everyone else the purpose of work will be instrumental, and the ends served by it will be those of their employer. In extending employment rights and improving employment conditions, governments and employers have done so from on high – their standpoint has been essentially superior. In struggling for new employment rights and better working conditions, employees and employee organisations have done so from below – their standpoint has been essentially subordinate. They have sought, and have achieved, improved security and protection for second-class citizens in a society in which they have been conditioned to accept the status of employee.

Rights raise the question of responsibilities. It would be cynical to say that rights are what people claim for themselves and responsibilities are what they impute to others. But there is an element of truth in this. In fact, the context in which new rights have normally been won is bound to encourage this way of thinking. Subordinates normally win new rights from superiors, and superiors are then regarded as responsible for safeguarding the new rights. The general tendency in late industrial society to be more concerned about rights than responsibilities is connected with the fact that most people now perceive themselves as dependent. We no longer feel capable of taking responsibility for meeting our own needs. We depend on shops to provide us with food, on the education profession to provide our children with learning, on the medical profession and the drug industry to provide us with health, on the state to provide us with welfare – and on employers to provide us with work. So, being dependent and perceiving ourselves subordinate, we claim rights to everything we need, and we perceive the people who manage the institutions of society – whoever they may be – as responsible for supplying it to us.

However, rights – like values, and the work ethic – evolve. In medieval times people thought that rights were determined by the hierarchical social and religious order then prevailing. By the 18th century the concepts of natural rights were coming in. The assumption was that rights existed objectively as part of the natural order, and that the use of reason could establish what they were. These concepts of natural law and natural rights underlay the American Declaration of Independence ('we hold these truths to be self-evident'), as well as the French Declaration of the Rights of Man. Today there is a further change. Our understanding of rights is becoming more subjective and developmental. We know that new rights develop and evolve from the actions of people who feel that the new rights should exist, and who then proceed to claim them and establish them by their own commitment and action.

There are signs that the next major extension in the field of rights may be the right to be responsible. This is perhaps especially apparent in the sphere of health – 'Whose Life Is It, Anyway?' – where people have already begun to claim the right to take decisions about their own medical treatment. More generally, Article 29(1) of the United Nations Universal Declaration of Human Rights comes near to declaring a right to be socially responsible, when it states that 'everyone has duties to the community in which alone the free and full development of his personality is possible'. In fact, the right to be responsible, that is the right to be a full-grown person, may well turn out to be one of the central, energising concepts of the post-industrial revolution. In the next few years it will certainly affect many people's attitudes to work, and their perceptions of what kinds of work are worth doing and how. It is a right that increasing numbers of people will not simply claim from their bosses or from the government. They will take action to establish it for themselves, by moving to work, or by organising work for themselves, which they regard as useful and valid. It could prove to be one of the most powerful factors in the transition to ownwork.

Depersonalisation

The idea of a right to be responsible involves a personalisation of work which, unfortunately, cuts right across the engrained thinking of the labour movement.

In Chapter 5 we saw that, as the Protestant work ethic evolved, it brought with it a shift in the bourgeois consciousness from a way of perceiving things personally to a way of perceiving them impersonally. The sense of mutual personal obligation between oneself and the people affected by one's activities was replaced by a sense of impersonal duty to do one's worldly work. That impersonal duty evolved into a simple drive to amass impersonal money-measurable wealth, and then into a sense of managing businesses – and society as a whole – as if they were impersonal machines.

In tune with the same spirit of the age, working-class consciousness became depersonalised also. As the bourgeoisie turned into impersonal servants of the state, so workers turned into impersonal instruments of their class. Proletarian depersonalisation followed from the dwindling sense of personal autonomy and the growing sense of personal dependency, experienced by working people as the industrial age progressed. As a modern Marxist writer explains, once the process of proletarianisation had stripped workers of all autonomous capacity to produce their own means of subsistence, the political imperatives of the class struggle prevented the labour movement from allowing the desire for personal autonomy to enter into their thinking.

> Autonomy is not a proletarian value . . . Being a proletarian implies that the only weapon you can turn against your exploiters is the quantity of interchangeable work and working power into which they have made you. The ideal militant is therefore the person most able to internalise this situation. He or she no longer exists as an autonomous individuality but is, instead, the impersonal representative of a class . . . The ideal militant must therefore repress his or her subjectivity and become the objective mouthpiece of the class . . . Rigidity, dogmatism, wooden language and authoritarianism are inherent qualities of such impersonal thinking devoid of subjectivity.[8]

The labour movement, and the socialist and Marxist strategies for change that were founded on it, came to take it for granted that work would continue to be organised impersonally as employment, and that society would continue to be governed impersonally by the state. In the course of the 19th century, the co-operative vision of men like Robert Owen that work might be organised as ownwork, and the vision of the utopian socialists that society might be so organised that people would take personal charge of their own lives in community, were left aside as little more than romantic dreams. Mainstream reformist thinking and mainstream revolutionary thinking in the labour movement became mechanistic and impersonal.

Reformist strategies have centred around the development of organised labour power – for example, by trades unions operating at the levels of the workplace, the firm, the industry, and the nation – to negotiate on workers' behalf with industry and government, both in the context of industrial relations and –through political parties like the Labour Party – in the wider political sphere. These strategies have had some success, within their self-imposed limits. They have been one of the factors which, over the last century and a half, have led to better conditions of employment and a better standard of living for employed people. But they have done little to help employed people to recover control over their work and a sense of responsibility for it. They have not been intended to do that.

Revolutionary strategies have centred around the development of organised labour power that would take over, rather than negotiate with, employing organisations and the state. Thus the syndicalists based their strategy on the aim of workers' councils taking over the organisation of production, factory by factory. 'All power to the Soviets' expressed the intention that workers should not only manage production, but should also organise the whole of social life. The strategy that shaped the Russian Revolution was for representatives of the proletariat directly to take over the state.

The syndicalist aim of taking power over production at the level of the place of employment was never successfully achieved on any scale, and – unless the Yugoslav system of self-management is regarded as an exception to this – has now lost its meaning as far as the mass of employees is concerned. Today, as André Gorz points out, 'workers' councils – which were the organs of working-class power when production was carried out by technically autonomous teams of workers – have become anachronistic in the giant factory of assembly lines and self-contained departments'. The factory itself is no longer an autonomous economic unit, but just one element in a larger production and marketing chain, dependent upon a centralised management co-ordinating dozens of productive units for its supplies, outlets, product lines, etc. The only power that employees can have within the framework of employment is a negative and subordinate sort – the power to resist the demands of management and to submit demands of their own.

The Leninist strategy of taking over the state in the name of the proletariat failed even more completely to give back to workers the power to control their work. As Trotsky put it, 'We oppose capitalist slavery by socially regulated labour on the basis of an economic plan, obligatory for the whole people and consequently compulsory for each worker in the country.' This involved 'the militarisation of labour' and 'the centralised distribution of labour-power in harmony with the general State plan'. The role of trade unions was not to struggle for better conditions of labour, but 'to organise the working class for the ends of production, to educate, discipline, distribute, group, retain certain categories and certain workers at their posts for fixed periods'. As Kolakowski says, Trotsky depicts the state of proletarian dictatorship 'as a huge permanent concentration camp in which the government exercises absolute power over every aspect of the citizens' lives and, in particular, decides how much work they shall do, of what kind and in what places. Individuals are nothing but labour units'.[9]

The depersonalisation of work had been taken to its extreme. It was a far cry from Marx's original vision of socialism as humanisation, a restoration of people's control over their own powers and their own creative energies, a 'return to a situation in which only individual human subjects truly exist and are not governed by any impersonal social force'.

Transformation of the Working Class
The working class came into existence in response to the new pattern of work, based on employment, brought in by the industrial revolution. It consisted of the great mass of people

whose work was needed and exploited by people more fortunate than themselves. Now, as the employment age comes to an end, what part is likely to be played by working people and the institutions of the labour movement in the transition to a new work order?

In his moving book, *Unemployment*, Jeremy Seabrook includes the following testimony to working-class values:[10]

> That practice, those values, the power of people to mitigate each other's suffering and console each other, to abate the worst visitations that either nature or their human oppressors can devise, constitute an abiding response to human existence itself. The way those people lived has a resonance and power that goes beyond the experience of the working class in one part of the world for a mere couple of centuries or so . . . The values which the old working class embodied in its resistance to the circumstances of life retain an inspirational, spiritual significance.

Today, however, the situation of many working people, and the nature of the working class as a whole, is quite different. People who have good jobs are now members of a privileged class. Acting through the trade unions and the labour movement they use their power, as middle-class professionals use theirs, to negotiate better deals for themselves. As employment continues to contract, the trade unions and the labour movement will find it very difficult not to fight to maintain the position of their well-established members. In doing so, for example by continuing to demand higher levels of pay and by taking industrial action with the aim of preserving existing jobs, they will probably help to accelerate the decline in employment.

The post-industrial counterpart to the proletariat of the mid-19th century will increasingly consist of the growing numbers of people who are unemployed, i.e. people whose work other people are no longer willing to organise and exploit, and whom the industrial-age ethic leaves feeling valueless, having nothing – not even their working-time – to sell. In *Farewell to the Working Class*, André Gorz describes this element of the old working class as a new 'non-class of non-workers', encompassing 'all those who have been expelled from production by the abolition of work, or whose capacities are underemployed as a result of the industrialisation of intellectual work'.

In their two books, *The Collapse of Work* and *The Leisure Shock*, Clive Jenkins and Barrie Sherman, writing from a progressive trade union point of view, argue that the work ethic must be replaced by a usefulness ethic and that the positive use of leisure time must be what provides the basis for usefulness. They foresee a future in which leisure and work will be indistinguishable and in which almost all work will be voluntary work, and they recognise that the need for less formal work raises fundamental challenges to all our systems. Their contribution to the debate is important. But they do not have a great deal to say about the role of the working class in the changes they foresee, or about the impact these changes will have on working-class values and outlook.

Jeremy Seabrook is pessimistic. He mourns the passing of the old working-class values. He finds, as one would expect, that people out of work are 'insulted by the rhetoric about leisure – it looks too much like futility'. But he is in no doubt that the solidarity and sharing, 'the living practice in the daily existence of millions of working people of the values of dignity, frugality, stoicism', have fallen victim to the blandishments of the consumer society and the welfare state. 'This has been the greatest loss of all because it means that the option of that alternative as something that could have grown organically out of the way people lived out their lives has been crushed. . . The damage to the function of the working class is profound and vast. It isn't confined to the work role, but to everything that stems from it, above all to its capacity to forge a more human alternative to capitalism.'

However that may be, André Gorz is quite clear that 'the priority task of the post-industrial Left' must be 'to extend self-motivated, self-rewarding activity', and he says that this 'expansion of the sphere of autonomy depends upon a freely available supply of convivial tools that allow individuals to do or make anything whose aesthetic or use-value is enhanced by doing it oneself'. Gorz speaks of the abolition of work and the need to ensure that the resulting availability of free time leads to the development of autonomous activity. For him 'the abolition of work does not mean abolition of the need for effort, the desire for activity, the pleasure of creation, the need to co-operate with others and be of some use to the community . . . the abolition of work means the freeing or liberation of time . . . so that individuals can exercise control over their bodies, their use of themselves, their choice of activity, their goals and productions'.

Although he calls it abolition of work, Gorz is talking about what I mean by ownwork. The important point, and here I agree with him, is that the post-industrial counterpart to the working-class movement of the early industrial age will be composed of people who cannot get jobs but have managed to liberate themselves from the job ethic – people for whom exclusion from employment has triggered a vision of a better society and a better future in which ownwork will be the norm. They will share this vision with the non-conforming middle-class people who, as I suggested in Chapter 5, deliberately choose to be independent of employment and to embrace the post-industrial ways of life that go with that independence.

In conclusion, therefore, the decline and accelerating breakdown of the industrial way of life and work is likely to affect in two different ways those who feel themselves to belong to the working-class tradition, just as it will affect in two different ways people who have tended to think of themselves as middle class.

First, there is every likelihood that the institutions of the labour movement, just like the institutions of conventional business and finance, will resist the transition to ownwork as strongly as they can. There is a danger here that the organised labour movement, while inadvertently helping to speed the loss of jobs and the long-term decline in employment, will call successfully on the working-class tradition of defensive solidarity in the face of change to resist the new work order that must take the place of employment. Millions of people could then find themselves stranded in a state of failed dependency on an old work order that is passing away in spite of all their efforts to cling to it. History would then repeat itself. The great structural changes in society brought by the post-industrial revolution would be almost as devastating for the unprepared, less privileged sections of society today as were the changes which the industrial revolution brought 200 years ago.

Second, however, there will be increasing numbers of

people who identify themselves with a working-class background, and whose exclusion from employment will begin to combine with a growing sense that there is a better way to live and work, less dependently, more personally, and more in tune with real needs. For them, the inspirational significance of the old working-class values of solidarity and mutual aid could have a very positive part to play in the transition to the new work ethic and the new ways of organising work. These values are, in fact, already clearly apparent in combination with a new sense of initiative, a new sense of responsibility and a new perception of real needs, in a number of inner city communities – such as those mentioned in Chapter 11 – which have decided to help themselves since no one else seems willing or able to do so.

Money

Money Now Dominant

Money plays the central role in late industrial society that religion played in the late middle ages. Then the local church was the most prominent building in most villages; today the prime sites in every high street are occupied by branches of banks, building societies and other financial concerns. The centres of medieval cities were dominated by cathedrals; today's city centres are dominated by the tower blocks of international banks. Today's army of accountants, bankers, taxpeople, insurance brokers, stock jobbers, foreign exchange dealers and countless other specialists in money, is the modern counterpart of the medieval army of priests, friars, monks, pardoners, summoners and other specialists in religious procedures and practices. The theologians of the late middle ages have their counterpart in the economists of the late industrial age. Financial mumbo-jumbo holds us in thrall today, as religious mumbo-jumbo held our ancestors then.

The expanding role of money in the lives of people and in the organisation of society has been a characteristic feature of the industrial age. It was people's growing dependence on paid labour, when they were deprived of access to land, that created the social conditions necessary for urban industrialism to flourish in the first place. In pre-industrial times people needed little money, because they provided most of the necessities of life for themselves and one another. Now, in late industrial society, people depend on either purchasing the necessities of life or being provided with them by public services paid for with public money.

The expansion of the role of money, then, was connected historically with the rise of employment. It was linked with the growing number of people who depended on money incomes from employment. Now the dominant form of work is paid work, and most people receive their incomes that way. They are either wage-earners or salary-earners themselves, or they are dependents of wage- and salary-earners. Those who receive no income or an insufficient income from paid work are eligible to receive an income from the state, in the form of unemployment or welfare benefits. But they are still regarded as unfortunate exceptions to the general rule. More fortunate exceptions, but exceptions nonetheless, are people who either earn an income from self-employment or receive an unearned income by way of interest or dividends on their own private capital.

As the role of money has become greater in the lives of people and society as a whole, the institutions set up to handle money have become bigger and more important. In step with increasing centralisation in industry and government, the financial institutions themselves have become more centralised. Small local banks, for example, were taken over by bigger banks and turned into local branches of national banking networks. Only in very exceptional cases are local financial institutions found today with the function of channelling local money into investment in support of local work.

The investment of money has thus become less personal and less local, as has the spending of it in supermarkets as contrasted with local corner shops, and the earning of it from faceless employing organisations. The impersonal character of investment has been reinforced by the industrial-age assumption that employing organisations will provide the capital assets – land, buildings, equipment and so forth – needed to support people's work. So, as increasing numbers of employees have acquired savings to invest, the assumption has been that they would not be interested in choosing to invest those savings to support their own or anyone else's work. Just as employees have been content to hand over responsibility to an employer to organise and control their work, so savers have been content to hand over responsibility to a bank, or a pension fund, or a building society, or some other financial institution, to control the use of their money.

Finally, as the role of money has become larger and larger in our lives, the possibilities have continually grown for making money out of money rather than out of useful work. The huge growth in money markets and other financial markets throughout the world has been one result of this. The ever-growing demand for capital assets like land and property, not only in order to use them but in the hope of selling them at a capital gain, has been another. This last, by raising the value of useful assets like land to artificial heights, has not only put them beyond the means of many people, thereby limiting their access to the physical capital they would need in order to work on their own account. It has also been one of many contributing factors to the massive expansion of borrowing and debt – personal, corporate, national and international – that has taken place in the last 40 years, and is perhaps the prime example of the growing dependence on money that now dominates most people's lives.

Possibilities for the Future
The characteristic features of how our use of money has developed during the industrial age thus include the following:

(1) The role of money in our lives, and the importance of finance and financial institutions in society, has continually grown.

(2) Most people's incomes have been directly linked with work, which has typically taken the form of paid employment.

(3) The capital assets needed for production and work have belonged to employers, and have been provided by them.

(4) Financial institutions have become more centralised, and less interested and less capable of providing channels for local investment in local work.

(5) People's attitude to their savings has become impersonal. People have become content to allow financial institutions to control the use to which their savings are put.

(6) The increasing switch of effort to making money out of money, and the expansion of debt that has come with it, mean that increasing numbers of people's work in the financial services industry has lost all direct connection with the meeting of real needs or with the provision of real goods and services.

Each of these industrial-age developments raises questions for the future. Will the role of money continue to grow – or has it reached its peak? Could it, perhaps, decline? Will people's incomes continue to depend on work – or will they, to a greater extent than now, become delinked from work? Will the capital base for production and work continue to be provided by employers – or will people increasingly provide it for their own work? Will financial institutions remain centralised – or will new institutions take shape for channelling local investment into local work? Will people continue to have an impersonal attitude towards their savings – or will they want a greater say in the uses to which their savings are put? Will the number of people employed in the financial services industry continue to grow – or may it perhaps contract?

The three different views of the future of work discussed in Chapter 1 give different answers to these questions. Some of these were touched on in Chapter 4.

The Business-As-Usual view assumes that money will continue to play a large part in our lives, and that most people's incomes will continue to be linked with their work. Full employment will be restored, partly by reducing average working hours and partly by replacing lost manufacturing jobs with new jobs in the service and information industries, including financial services. The capital needed for production and work will continue to be provided by employers. People's attitude to their savings, and the structure and aims of the financial services industry, will remain much as they are today.

The HE vision of the future foresees money playing an even larger part in most people's lives than it does today. People will have more leisure, and will need more money to spend on it. Moreover, many essential activities which people still do today unpaid – such as parenting, housekeeping, comforting, preparing meals, looking after children and elderly people, providing hospitality at home to friends – will be transformed into paid work. Either the same people will be paid for doing these things who now do them unpaid, or these activities will be replaced by commercial and professional services. In the first case, parents and housewives and househusbands will be paid for carrying out their functions. In the second, meals will no longer be prepared at home, but brought in or eaten out; professional bereavement counsellors will replace relatives and friends as a source of comfort and support in time of need; and so on. So people will have to pay, either directly or through taxation, for many services which today we still provide free for ourselves and one another. Money will thus play an even larger part in our lives than it does today.

Where does the HE vision see people getting the extra money from to pay for all this? This is not always very clear. Sometimes HE proponents seem to fall back on a Business-As-Usual approach: the link between incomes and work will be maintained; incomes will rise as new jobs get created and as more people get paid for activities they now do unpaid; so, in general, people will be able to buy more goods and services and pay more taxes. But often, as we suggested in Chapter 4, the HE vision implies the opposite of this: the necessary work of society will be done by a smaller and smaller number of experts, and the rest of the population will live lives of leisure. The link between work and income will be broken for most people. They will need a new source of income in the shape of a Guaranteed Basic Income(GBI). But, as we saw in Chapter 4, there would be difficulties about this in a HE future.

So far as the other questions are concerned, the HE vision implies that the financial structure of society stays much as it is today only more so. Ever larger amounts of investment will continue to be channelled into ever larger and more capital-intensive projects controlled by ever fewer people. The centralisation and impersonality of the financial system will become even more marked. Ever greater emphasis will be placed on making money out of money, as electronic systems of transferring money make it possible for money to be switched instantaneously from any account in any part of the world to any other.

Money and Ownwork
The SHE view, of a future in which a shift from employment to ownwork is an important trend, gives different answers to these questions.

As we have seen, it envisages a post-employment society, in which the stark choice between employment and unemployment, work and leisure, will increasingly be replaced by a wide range of flexible options for work and useful activity, including part-time employment, self-employment, irregular and casual employment, co-operative and community work, voluntary work, do-it-yourself activities, and productive leisure, as well as full-time employment. This shift towards ownwork implies a shift towards self-help, mutual aid, and household and local self-sufficiency, together with some lessening of dependency on goods and services which are either purchased directly or are paid for at public expense. In contrast with the HE vision, the SHE vision thus foresees some substitution of *unpaid* activity for *paid* activity, and therefore some decline in the role of money in our lives. It also foresees that unpaid work will be valued more highly than today, and consequently that there will be some further weakening of the present link between employment and income.

A shift towards ownwork will not, of course, imply that people will stop using money altogether in post-industrial society, any more than people lost all concern for religion when the middle ages came to an end. Nor will it imply that in post-industrial society people will altogether stop earning money from work. It merely implies that the continuing expansion of the role of money and of financial institutions in our lives will cease, and that the link between money incomes and work will become weaker for more and more people.

This weakening of the link between income and work will be achieved by extending today's entitlements to unemployment and social security benefits and other transfer payments. Whereas today these payments provide an income to particular categories of people – pensioners and the unemployed, for example – who do not earn a sufficient income from work, the transfer payments system would be extended to provide a GBI to all citizens unconditionally, regardless of what work they do, if any. Chapter 4 contained a preliminary discussion of the GBI idea. A fuller discussion will be found in Chapter 12.

It will not, however, be only for the distribution of income that new arrangements will have to be made. As ownwork becomes more widespread, the distribution of capital will be affected. Many more people than today will need access to the physical and financial capital needed to support their work. A post-industrial society in which ownwork is the norm will have to discard the industrial-age assumption that it is for employers to provide the capital needed for work. It will increasingly be for people themselves to possess and have access to these capital assets, including land, either as individuals working on their own account or as members of co-operating groups. A new approach to distributing capital will be just as important as a new approach to distributing income.

One aspect of this new approach to distributing capital will affect the control of savings, and the channels through which investment is made. We have already noted that, in the industrial age, just as people have become conditioned to give control of their work to employers, so they have become conditioned to give control of their savings to financial institutions. Just as people have allowed employers to decide on the purposes to which their work will be put, so they have been content to allow banks and other financial institutions to decide on the purposes to which their savings will be put. People have been content to relinquish the vital power to use their own money on projects which they themselves value. All they have asked is that they receive the going rate of monetary return by way of dividends or interest, and that the capital value of their savings be maintained. In post-industrial society, however, just as the SHE vision foresees employment being largely replaced by ownwork, so it foresees a rising demand for new channels of investment which will enable people to direct their money into projects that reflect their own preferences and choices, including projects of their own. Today's 'socially responsible investment' initiatives, that enable investors to avoid investing in industries, countries or projects they dislike, such as armaments, South Africa and nuclear power, are a step in this direction. But new channels will also be needed which will positively enable people to invest in specific types of preferred projects, such as renewable energy, alternative technology or community enterprises.[1]

The spread of ownwork will mean that, not just individual people, but local communities too, will increasingly demand to use their money on projects that serve needs and preferences of their own. The financial system and financial institutions that have developed in late industrial society make little provision for the reinvestment of locally generated money in local projects and local initiatives. Just as local work has increasingly come under the control of national and multinational companies and government agencies based elsewhere, so local money has increasingly been channelled, through national financial institutions located elsewhere, into projects that have no connection with local purposes and needs. New channels will be needed through which local capital can be invested in local work.[2]

The growing desire of people to direct their spare money into projects of their own choice will in part be a growing desire to invest their money in local economic and social enterprises which will help to improve the locality in which they themselves live, and help to put it on a satisfactory and stable economic and social base. It will thus directly reinforce the shift towards greater local economic self-reliance more generally. The personal and local thrust of ownwork will thus help to modify the impersonal outlook and centralised institutional structure on which the present financial system is based.

Just as the shift towards ownwork will tend to reduce the present dependence of individuals and households on earning and spending money, so investment in local work to meet local needs will tend to reduce the dependence of localities on earning money from outside employers in order to spend it on imports from outside suppliers, and to increase the local circulation of local money. This will not only be a good indicator of the improving health of the local economy. It will also tend to redirect activity into what are personally and locally perceived as real needs, and away from impersonal efforts simply to make more money out of money regardless of the value of the activities generated thereby.

Positive and Negative Effects
Thus, as the post-industrial revolution gathers pace and brings an expansion of ownwork with it, there will be both positive and negative consequences for the present system of money and finance.

On the positive side, the growth of ownwork will create a growing demand for access to personally controlled capital to support it, as well as a growing demand for advice on the financial management of ownwork. This is likely to include advice on ways of living better on less money, on the pros and cons of investing capital to support ownwork that reduces the need for subsequent spending and therefore for subsequent earning, and on the right balance between paid and unpaid work, and between purchased consumption and self-produced goods and services.

Also on the positive side, the growth of local financial and economic self-reliance will create a growing demand for channels through which to invest local funds locally. New local financial institutions will spring up all over the place, and will have to be properly managed.

But this growth of new financial services and institutions at the personal and local level will be paralleled by a decline elsewhere.

For example, if paid employment ceases to grow and goes into a steady decline, the regular flow of money into pension funds in the form of pension contributions will also cease to grow and will go into decline. The funds available to pension funds for investment will fall off. Not only will the role of pension funds themselves be affected. The demand for – and therefore the value of – the things that pension funds invest in, that is to say equities, gilt-edged stock and property, will also be affected.[3] Again, to take a second example, if more people spend more of their time and energy working to build or part-build their own houses, and less time and energy working for employers for pay, the demand for mortgage money for home-buying and the ability to pay off such mortgages will decline. The role of the building societies in borrowing money and lending it for house purchase will also decline. Again, thirdly, if more local money circulates locally instead of through national and international channels, the cash flows handled by national and international institutions will fall, their role will decline, and the capital values of the kind of investments into which they channel money will tend to fall too. Localities, like people, will become less dependent on the services of outside financial institutions.

These three examples illustrate the general point. A significant shift from employment to ownwork will bring a decline in the use of money by households. A significant shift to greater local economic self-reliance will bring a decline in the circulation of money between different localities. These two developments together will mean a significant decline in, or at least a significant slowing down in the growth of, the flow of money through society at national and international levels.

This will call in question the position of many of today's

financial institutions whose viability depends on the expectation of continually rising cash flows. It will also call in question many of today's capital values, e.g. of commercial properties and agricultural land, which also reflect the expectation of continually rising cash flows and rates of return. Finally, it will call in question the solvency of many people and organisations, and also nation states, whose ability to pay off their present levels of indebtedness (and even to service their present debts) depends on the expectations of continually rising money incomes based on continually rising cash flows.[4] Thus, among other things, it could increase the likelihood of an international banking collapse, already threatened by the inability of many third world nations to repay their present crippling levels of debt to western banks.

A 'Dissolution of the Monasteries'?

Money, as I have said, has played the central role in late industrial societies that religion played in the late middle ages. People's lives in societies like ours have revolved around money, as people's lives in medieval society revolved around religion. Money has been among our main worries, as religion was among theirs. Great institutions and a wide range of professions and sub-professions have grown up to handle money on behalf of the dependent majority, as formerly they grew up around religion. Ambitious men have based their search for power on money, as formerly they based it on religion. Just as the ecclesiastical and monastic institutions of the late middle ages came to be regarded as exercising unaccountable power, so today's financial institutions are widely seen to exercise great power, for example in the creation of credit, in the allocation of investment funds, and in their effect on society as a whole, without being properly accountable or under social control. In principle, as I have argued elsewhere,[5] the monetary and financial system could be and should be one of society's most effective mechanisms of social choice, a scoring system openly and fairly allocating purchasing power to people according to their entitlement and giving them freedom to use it as they choose, and an allocation system for distributing resources and investment where they are most needed. In practice, it is nothing of the sort.

The dissolution of the monasteries was an event that clearly

marked the decline of religion in the transition from medieval
to modern times. May the post-industrial counterpart to that
event prove to be a monetary and financial collapse so severe
that governments will have no option but to take direct control
of the monetary and financial system? Such a collapse might
be precipitated by a combination of: an international banking
breakdown; a collapse of agricultural land values following
withdrawal of today's high levels of agricultural support from
public funds, as under the Common Agricultural Policy in
Europe; a collapse of industrial and commercial property
values, following recognition that conventional forms of
economic growth and conventional levels of cash flow growth
will not come back; and growing awareness that increasing
numbers of financial institutions, like pension funds, as well
as ordinary businesses and individuals, may be unable to meet
their obligations. The most likely date for such a collapse, to
be followed by a government takeover and subsequently by
financial decentralisation and reform, is probably the early
1990s when the current Kondratieff downwave nears its
trough. There is little doubt in my mind that at least some later
historians would look back on such an event as marking the
end of the era which we call the industrial age.

It will, I hope, prove possible to avoid a disastrous collapse
of that kind. But the institutions of money and finance have
been a central part of the whole empire of organisations and
institutions and professions that have grown up in the industrial age, and on which the citizens of industrialised countries
have become dependent. If the end of that empire is now
drawing near, urgent questions must be faced. What must we
do to liberate ourselves from our present dependence on
money and financial institutions, so that their decline and
possible collapse will leave us comparatively unscathed? How
should those who manage these institutions manage their
decline? How should they set about decolonising their present empire in good order, and so forestall the possible
calamity of its disorderly collapse?

Politics and Government

The dominant forms of politics and government today are part of the social structure of the employment age. Today's mass political parties and government bureaucracies are products of the factory mentality. The growing formalisation of politics and government over the last 200 years reflects the growing formalisation of work as employment. We have become dependent on professional politicians to do our politics for us, just as we have become dependent on employers to organise our work. In their turn, our government employees and career politicians have become dependent on politics and government to provide them with their work and livelihood.

How, then, will the existing forms of politics and government be affected by the transition to ownwork? And what part are they likely to play in helping the transition to come about, or in hindering it?

Political Alignments during the Industrial Age
It is quite clear that changes in the prevailing pattern of work in society tend to be followed, some time after the event, by corresponding shifts in political alignment. This is natural enough, since both the prevailing pattern of work and the prevailing political alignment are connected with the distribution of power in society. Here is a brief account of the two main political shifts that took place in Britain during the industrial age.

When most people still worked on the land, the main political divide was between Tories and Whigs. Both represented landed interests. The Tories represented the interests of the monarchy and the rural squirearchy, and the Whigs represented the interests of the landed aristocracy. The first shift took place when work moved away from the land into manu-

137

facturing industry in the cities. The old political opposition
between Tories and Whigs was then replaced by a new opposition: the Tories were transformed into Conservatives, representing the whole agricultural and landed interest
(including the interest of the big aristocratic land-owners); and
the Whigs were replaced by the Liberals, representing the new
urban manufacturing interest. That realignment took place in
the politically turbulent years of mid-19th century Britain,
roughly between 1830 and 1860.

The second shift in political alignment, completed about 60
years later in the mid-1920s, reflected the emergence of formally organised employment as the dominant form of work:
the Conservatives now sought to represent the interests of all
employers, industrial as well as agricultural; and Labour, representing the combined interests of all employees, replaced
the Liberals as the main opposition to the Conservatives.

These two structural realignments in politics that took place
during the industrial age were fairly and squarely based on
shifts in the relative importance of land, capital and labour,
the three traditional factors of production around which the
economic thinking of the industrial age has revolved. The
Tory-versus-Whig alignment matched the dominance of land.
Then, reflecting the growing importance of industrial and
financial capital, the Conservative-versus-Liberal alignment
matched the conflict between the old landed interest and the
new capitalist interest. Then, again, reflecting the growing
importance of labour and the new perception of land as just
one form of capital, the Conservative-versus-Labour alignment matched the conflict between capital (including land
ownership) and labour.

Possible Futures for Politics and Government
It may be possible to show that some connection exists between the successive long waves of economic prosperity and
decline – the Kondratieff cycles discussed in Chapter 2 – and
the successive shifts from one structure of political alignment
to another, that have taken place during the industrial age. In
that case, we might perhaps find that the next political shift is
due within the next five or ten years.

However that may be, as we think now about the future of
politics and government, the industrial-age experience does

suggest some questions. First, has any new factor of production recently emerged whose importance could override the existing capital-versus-labour alignment? Second, will the link between political alignment and factors of production continue to hold? Or will it prove to have been valid only in the production-oriented culture of the industrial age? Third, will the processes of politics and government in the post-industrial period continue to be cast in the institutional mould they have acquired during the industrial age?

Keeping these questions in mind, let us now explore what the three views of the future – Business As Usual, HE and SHE – could imply for the future of politics and government.

The Business-As-Usual view is the view held by most Conservative and Labour supporters. They assume that institutionalised politics will continue to be the norm, and that the main political division will continue to be based on the dominant work patterns of the late industrial age. In other words, they assume that employment will remain the dominant form of work and that the prevailing political alignment will continue to reflect the conflict of interest between 'the two sides of industry', capital and labour, employer and employee. They assume, if they ever think about it, that ownwork will remain a utopian dream for the vast majority of people; and, as they begin to realise that ownwork could be a possibility for growing numbers of people, their automatic reaction will be to resist it.

The HE view of the future perceives that the present political alignment is out of date and that its replacement by a new one is due – or overdue. It maintains that for many years, knowledge and skill – including managerial and professional expertise – have been just as important a factor of production as capital and labour. The emergence of this new factor of production has been paralleled by the emergence of the services and information industries as the sector of work most typical of late industrial society. It has been reflected in the rise of a new class of scientists, engineers, managers, experts, professionals, service technicians and organisation men, whose economic and political interests are neither those of capital nor those of old-fashioned labour.[1]

In some countries the structure of politics began to respond to this change many years ago. In Sweden and West Germany, for example, the rise of the new class and the importance of their field of work has been reflected in the emergence of Social Democratic parties and governments. But in Britain, among other countries, the corresponding shift in the structure of politics has hardly yet begun.

Eventually, the political realignment that would go with the transition to a HE future would no doubt reflect the emerging division of society between the minority who would design and plan and manage and operate a capital-intensive economy, and the majority of leisured consumers and dependents to whom they would provide goods and services. The new line-up would be between politicians representing the interests of the two main factors of production – skilled managerial and technical workers, and capital – on the one side, and politicians representing consumer and welfare and environmental interests on the other.

Signs of a possible coalition between all the main factors of production could be seen in the drift towards closer co-operation between government, industry and trade unions that took place in Britain in the 1960s and 1970s with the establishment of bodies like the National Economic Development Council (NEDC), and which has been taken rather further in the economic planning arrangements that now exist in countries like Sweden, France, Japan and Germany. At the same time, in all the industrialised countries there have been unmistakeable signs that pressure groups and action groups, representing consumer, welfare and environmental interests against production interests, are moving towards closer cooperation with one another.[2]

But, while the HE view implies a new *alignment* in politics, and an alignment based on production-versus-consumption interests, rather than on one production interest versus another, it implies no real change in the *processes* of politics and government. The institutionalisation of politics and government during the industrial age already reflects the basic structure of a HE society, split between a managerial and professional elite on the one hand and the rest of the population on the other. Politics and government have already become services (or, if you prefer, commodities), provided by cadres of professional politicians and bureaucrats with privileged access to information and communication channels, to the rest of us political drones whose participation in politics consists mainly of watching television, reading newspapers and casting our votes from time to time.

The SHE vision of a society in which ownwork will be the norm foresees, as does the HE vision, a shift to a new political alignment no longer based on the conflict of interest between employers and employees. But it goes further than that. It foresees, as the HE vision does not, a radical change in the political process itself. The SHE vision foresees that politics, like work, will increasingly become an activity which people take charge of and organise for themselves. This implies a shift away from national representative politics and centralised bureaucratic government to direct, participatory politics and government at local and neighbourhood levels. It implies that people will take more control over all the decisions that affect their lives, as well as over the work they do. It implies a deinstitutionalisation of politics, just as the shift from employment to ownwork implies a deinstitutionalisation of work. It is likely to be resisted, not only by the political representatives of capital and labour, and by those of the skilled managerial and technical interest, but by professional politicians and government officials generally, regardless of their particular political stance. After all, their own positions depend on a continuation of the existing processes and institutions of politics and government, and on the continued assumption that their kind of employment remains the best way to do their kind of work.

A Scenario

History shows that changes in political alignments, and changes in government policies, take place some time after the changes in the dominant pattern of work which they reflect. The existing power structure, based on the pattern of work that is on the way out, resists the consequences of change as long as it can. Political structure adapts to changes in work structure only after a time-lag.

A good 19th-century example of this is the repeal of the Corn Laws. By restricting imports into Britain, the Corn Laws had kept up the price of home-grown corn. This had served the interests of a predominantly agricultural society, in which most people worked on the land. But it raised the price of food for urban industrial workers, and was contrary to the interests of an industrialising society. The dominant political parties of the time, Whigs and Tories, both had their power base in the old agricultural interest, and contrived to put off repealing the Corn Laws until 1846, by which time the industrialisation of Britain was already far advanced. And it was not until later even than that, that the old Tory-versus-Whig line-up in British politics finally broke down, to be replaced by Conservatives versus Liberals.

In the same way today the Conservative and Labour interests try to preserve a structure of politics based on capital versus labour, employers versus employees, long after this has ceased to match the actual pattern of work in society – which already involves most people, including most 'top people', being employed in professionally managed organisations rather than by capital-owning employers. This structural inertia is strengthened by the fact that most leading people in all walks of life, together with their juniors who hope to follow them up the career ladders of business, government, trade unions and the professions, owe their positions and their prospects of further advancement to the structures thrown up by a society in which employment has been the dominant form of work. So they too tend to resist the transition to a post-employment way of work and life.

By refusing to recognise that a historic transition from an agricultural to an industrial society was taking place, the Whigs and Tories and the rest of the early-19th-century establishment caused unnecessary hardship to the growing number of urban industrial workers who then represented the wave of the future. Just so, the various sections of today's establishment are causing hardship to the growing number of people who now represent the wave of the future – those who don't have jobs – by refusing to recognise that an equally historic transition is taking place from the age of employment to a new work order. They will almost certainly continue to do so until they are compelled to recognise that the old work order has broken down.

Then, as the prospect of restoring full employment fades away, a choice will present itself between the work pattern offered by the HE vision (a two-class society split between managerialist workers and workless drones) and the work pattern offered by the SHE vision (ownwork as the norm). The consequent political realignment may then tend to take shape broadly as follows. On the one side will be those mainstream elements in the Conservative, Labour and Social Democrat traditions which are rooted in the institutions of late industrial society and its Business-As-Usual and hyper-expansionist tendencies. On the other side will be the alternative, decentralising elements in those three parties, together with many Liberal and Ecology Party supporters and people of no party-political allegiance. The first side will be a broadly conservative grouping: representing managerialist, trade unionist, financial, professional and other organisational interests; supporting continuing centralisation and dominant/dependent social and economic relationships; and reflecting institutional values. The second will be a broadly radical grouping: representing consumers, welfare and environmental interests and the decentralist aspirations of local communities; supporting the spread of self-reliance and mutual aid in place of dependence on institutions; and reflecting personal values.

The first of these two realigned groupings will not question the existing processes of representative politics and bureaucratic government. It will simply set itself to manage them.

For the more radical grouping, however, things will not be so simple. On the one hand it will contain conventional politicians and pressure-groupers. Their main aims will be to create new structures of power representing consumer, welfare, local and environmental interests in the existing political arena, and to force through changes in existing public policies. Personally, many of them will be pursuing a more or less conventional career in professional politics and government. Although they will be eager to represent the new post-industrial coalition of interests, they will be eager to do so through the old political processes.

On the other hand, the new radical coalition will also contain people who perceive the existing processes of centralised, institutional politics and government as part of the problem – a powerful obstacle to creating the new structural relationships in society which will enable people to take more control over their lives and work. Such people will want to promote withdrawal from dependence on institutionalised politics and government, as a key element in a strategy of social change which will also involve withdrawal from dependence on employment as the accepted way of organising work. For them it will be a top priority to supplement and eventually to replace the existing political and governmental processes with new post-industrial forms of politics and government based on personal and local activity, just as it will be a top priority to replace conventional jobs with new post-industrial ways of working.[3]

This division within the radical movement in the transition to a post-industrial society will have 19th-century echoes. Then, in the transition to the new industrial society, there was a comparable division between the rising middle-class and working-class interests within the radical movement. Then the division was between parliamentary reformers who wanted the new industrial interests to be effectively represented in the existing political system, and people like the Chartists who wanted a much more fundamental restructuring of society.[4] The division now is going to be between those who want the new post-industrial interests to be effectively represented through the existing political system, and those who believe these new interests require a more fundamental restructuring of society – including deinstitutionalisation of the system of politics and government itself.

Collapse or Decolonisation
Thus the political and governmental context in which the transition towards ownwork will take place is bound to be uncertain and shifting, obstructive and unreliable. Not only will the transition to ownwork be resisted by those with a direct interest in keeping employment as the dominant form of work. But because ownwork will imply an increase in personal and local autonomy in a political as well as an economic sense, the transition to it will also be resisted by those with a vested interest in the existing processes of representative politics and bureaucratic government. Only when the prospect of breakdown, both of employment as the main way to organise work and of existing forms of politics and government as the main way to run our affairs, begins to loom large, will resistance to the idea of ownwork begin to soften. Only when the collapse of an empire begins to seem imminent, does orderly decolonisation come to be seen as a desirable goal.

Once that stage is reached, however, new opportunities open up for those who have prepared themselves to play a positive part in the decolonisation process. At that point the coming decolonisation of work will offer growing opportunities for achievement and success to those politicians and public officials who have prepared themselves for the transition to ownwork, who have thought out the changes it will require, and who are able to introduce and carry them out. The same will be true for people in the organised labour movement and the financial system (see Chapters 8 and 9), and also for people with responsibility for personnel management in employing organisations. What all this will mean in practice is discussed in Part 4.

PART 4

PRACTICALITIES OF THE TRANSITION

The transition to ownwork has already begun. Chapter 11 shows that many practical responses to the unemployment crisis in the last few years can be seen as steps in this direction.

As more people come to see things this way, the pace of transition will speed up. But some people will not see things this way, and some – especially in positions of power and influence based on the status quo – will positively resist the change. So the transition will not be planned and managed systematically from above. It will rather be an organic process of transformation from below, as the old way of organising work as employment continues to break down, and new ways of organising it as ownwork continue to break through.

An ownwork agenda is outlined in Chapter 12. Although this may suggest some planks for a political platform of the conventional kind, its main aims are rather different: first, to encourage sympathetic readers to take part in creating a better future for work, as they decide on their own initiative without waiting for politicians and governments to give a lead; and, second, to enable readers who are less committed but nonetheless interested in the future, to understand the kinds of things that a transition to ownwork would involve if it should come about.

11

The Shift to Ownwork
Has Already Begun

Much of the response to the unemployment crisis so far has been based on the assumption that conventional employment will remain the norm and that full employment is still a feasible goal. This is true of individual people, employers, and agencies of local and central government, as well as trade unions and the education and planning professions, not to mention other institutions and professions like finance and the law which are hardly aware that important changes in patterns of work may be taking place. So in the mid-1980s most people still feel they should continue to look for jobs; progressive employers still try to find new jobs for their redundant employees, and support schemes to create new job opportunities in areas badly affected by their redundancies; increasing numbers of local authorities are adopting policies aimed at creating local jobs; central government still continues to give out large sums of money to employers with the aim of creating new jobs; and Manpower Service Commission schemes aim to provide people with something to do until they can find a job, and to give young people the kind of work experience and training that will prepare them eventually to get a job.

But although conventional employment has remained the theoretical goal, in practice much of what has been happening points towards a new future in which personal and local ownwork will play an increasingly important part. When future historians look back from the mid-21st century in 60 or 70 years' time, they will see that there had already taken place by the mid-1980s the first, hesitant, largely unconscious phase of the shift to a new post-industrial work order in which personal and local ownwork eventually became no longer marginal alternatives to conventional employment, but themselves came to occupy centre stage.

Personal Ownwork

The last few years have seen a growth of initiatives on the part of individual people, aiming to achieve greater personal autonomy in their work. Sometimes these initiatives are taken by choice, and sometimes they are due to compulsion – as a result of losing or not being able to get a job. They often happen from a mixture of choice and compulsion. An increasing number of people, sometimes only half-consciously, wish to make the kind of change in their way of living and working that will allow them to be less dependent on employment, but – whether because of family obligations or the psychic investment they have already put into their job or, more simply, because of timidity and lack of energy and will – they are reluctant to make the change on their own decision and responsibility. As I know from my own experience ten years ago, they do not feel strong enough to take the initiative themselves or sufficiently justified in making the change until it is forced upon them. When it is forced upon them, for example by redundancy or because of conflict with their employer, they find it possible to accept what has happened, and sometimes even to welcome it as giving them an opportunity to branch out on their own.

At present these may only be the fortunate few. But as public discussion and debate have continued to mount about the future of work, and as people have talked to one another about their own work problems and aspirations, a consciousness-raising process has been taking place. People, especially unemployed people, who have hitherto assumed they were powerless to decide and define the purposes of their work, have discovered – as they have shared their hopes and their fears and their time with one another – that they have much more power in this respect than they thought. They have discovered self-organised activities that are worth doing, and they have begun to seek information, advice and counselling about possible openings for activities of that kind. They have begun to look for conditions of employment (e.g. part-time work or early retirement) which will leave them with more time and energy for projects of their own. People have been increasingly helped to do this by the example, and often by the more direct assistance, of other individuals and groups who have already made the change from unsatisfactory employment (or unemployment) to valuable and rewarding ownwork.[1]

One example of the shift to ownwork at the personal level is the rise in self-employment. In Britain self-employment is now growing at a rate of about 5% a year. A growing number of courses for prospective entrepreneurs is being provided by such organisations as the Manchester Business School and URBED (Urban Economic Development). There is a growing demand for books and publications which help and encourage people to set themselves up in business. The Manpower Services Commission has a scheme which helps unemployed people to start up in business on their own by, in effect, paying them a salary for a start-up period, provided that they have a good business idea and can raise £1000 capital.

The entrepreneurial way of work attracts a number of different kinds of people. There are conventional capitalist entrepreneurs who are attracted by the prospect of building up a conventional business and making a lot of money for themselves. There are lifestyle entrepreneurs who are attracted by the prospect of freedom and the opportunity to do their own thing. And there are social entrepreneurs whose flair and drive and commitment are attracted by the new local ownwork initiatives discussed below.[2]

Other signs of the shift to personal ownwork are: the rise in part-time jobs, now nearly 20% of the total number of jobs, which enable people – men, as well as women – to have more time to devote to their families and to projects of their own; the increasing number of men and women who retire from employment early, and involve themselves in voluntary work of their own choice; the increasing number of men who are deciding to work at home as househusbands, while their wives take on the task of breadwinner going out to work; and the increasing number of people who are adopting a rather more self-sufficient lifestyle, substituting their own unpaid work to provide for some of their own needs in place of earning money to spend on meeting those needs by working in paid employment.

The sense of personal powerlessness and futility experienced by many unemployed people is one of the most damaging effects of the present crisis of work. A vital part in counteracting this is now being played by unemployment cen-

tres and groups of local voluntary associations which have
come into existence in many parts of countries like Britain in
the last few years. Among other things, they are helping unemployed people to get together and organise work for themselves. Thereby they are helping to establish the new kinds of
small local enterprise in which increasing numbers of people
are likely to work as the post-industrial transition to ownwork
gathers pace. This takes us across the broad, rather blurred
dividing line between personal and local ownwork.

Local Ownwork
Tremendous changes have taken place over the last 10 or 15
years in our perceptions of local enterprise and the local
economy. At every level the importance of local employment
initiatives is now accepted, to an extent that would have been
unthinkable as recently as the 1960s. Voluntary associations,
businesses, local authorities, agencies of central government,
and supranational organisations such as the European
Economic Commission (EEC) and the Organisation for
Economic Cooperation and Development (OECD), are all now
deeply involved.

Local voluntary initiatives to counteract unemployment
have sprung up in many places in countries like Britain in the
last few years. They include self-help groups of unemployed
managers and professionals, centres for unemployed people
set up by the trade union movement, similar centres set up by
the churches and by co-operative associations of local voluntary groups, and a wide variety of relatively autonomous skill
exchanges and other groups of unemployed people who have
come together for mutual support. They have been backed
nationally by an increasing number of organisations such as
the National Council for Voluntary Organisations (NCVO), the
British Unemployment Resource Network (BURN), Church
Action With The Unemployed (CAWTU), The Volunteer Centre,
and the Unemployment Initiatives Service of the Scottish
Community Education Centre and its newspaper, *SCAN*.

One of the most significant outcomes of the growing voluntary response to local unemployment has been the rise of
community businesses and community enterprises. This new
approach to economic self-help in areas of high unemploy-

ment which are unattractive to conventional profit-making businesses recognises a threefold objective: to run an economically viable enterprise; to provide local work; and to provide goods and services to meet local needs. In helping to formulate this new approach, the Gulbenkian Foundation, in two 1982 reports on 'Whose Business Is Business?' and 'Community Business Works', saw community business ventures as having the potential to develop into a third arm of enterprise alongside private enterprise and public enterprise, in the way that non-profit housing associations form a third arm of housing alongside the private housing sector and the public housing sector.

Among outstanding examples of community enterprises have been the Craigmillar Festival Society in Edinburgh and the Easterhouse Festival Society in Glasgow, both of which have developed into community conglomerates, not only organising festivals and other cultural and sporting events but also shops, construction teams, workshops, and other business endeavours that serve the local community. The Pleck Community in Walsall is another community conglomerate, embracing community housing management, toy manufacturing, vehicle repair, and food-growing among its wide range of activities. The community conglomerate is likely to be an important part of the pattern for the future. But at the same time many specific types of community businesses will continue to spring up, such as community farms, community workshops, community shops, and community services of all kinds.

The rise of community businesses has been paralleled by the growing interest in common ownerships and co-operatives over the last 10 or 15 years. Co-operatives and common ownerships are owned and controlled by the people who work in them, whereas community businesses are not necessarily structured that way. For the future, two points have to be taken into account. First, it has to be accepted that much of the interest in co-operatives that surfaced in the 1970s was backward-looking – a politically motivated interest or, in some cases, a theoretical academic interest in the conversion to worker ownership of inefficient and often bankrupt concerns which had never been set up with the aim of meeting local community needs, whose products and objectives therefore failed to engage the full commitment of the workers and their families and neighbours, and which therefore seemed artificially contrived. Second, it has to be recognised that the co-operative or common ownership structure will not always be suitable for community businesses, especially in the early stages of their existence. Many of the existing community businesses are, in fact, companies limited by guarantee with charitable status. Nonetheless, there is no doubt that the co-operative or common ownership structure is likely to prove a suitable structure for many community businesses once they are established on an economically viable footing.

Community businesses, co-operatives and common ownerships are just three specific examples of many different forms of enterprise structure found among local concerns, ranging from the wholly commercial small business to the wholly charitable activity or to the public service agency wholly funded by the taxpayer. At other intermediate points are many different types of enterprises with social and amenity objectives (including conservation and preservation), as well as economic and commercial objectives. As local initiatives develop further and local economies take on a larger role, it will become increasingly important to clarify which legal and financial structures are best suited to which kinds of enterprise at which particular stages of their development. To take just one illustrative example, the Ironbridge Gorge Museum Trust is the organisation which runs the industrial history and industrial arechaeology museums at and near the famous Iron Bridge over the river Severn in Shropshire – the first iron bridge ever built (in 1779) and now a symbol of the industrial revolution. Those museums are staffed by a range of different types of people, including full-time professional employees, part-time employees, unemployed people working on Manpower Service Commission projects, and 'friends' who man the museum exhibits as volunteers and act as guides for visitors. The museums are financed from a similarly wide range of sources, including individual subscriptions, visitors' entrance fees, sales in the museum shops, grants from central and local government, and funds raised from business and industry. One of the questions for the future for this and many comparable organisations playing a significant part in local economies is: what patterns of staffing and financing should they develop? What mix of the different types of people and what mix of the different sources of funds will be best for them to adopt? Putting the same question more broadly, what kinds of organisation should they try to develop into? How should they define their role as part of the local economies in which they operate?

In support of community business and other forms of local enterprise, there have grown up in the last five or ten years various kinds of local development agencies. In some cases these are specific to the type of enterprise which they support, like Co-operative Development Agencies or the Industrial Common Ownership Movement in Britain. In other cases they are local development agencies in a more general sense, like Local Enterprise Trusts in Britain and Boutiques de Gestion in France. In either case they exist to provide advice and services, in particular in the spheres of staffing and finance, to enterprises calling on them for support. A number of other advisory centres have also sprung up, such as the Centre for Employment Initiatives in London, and Strathclyde Community Business and the Planning Exchange and its Local Economic Development Information Service (LEDIS), both of which are in the Glasgow area. Many of these organisations are supported by local government, and big companies, and other big business organisations such as banks.

In contrast with this ad hoc growth of local economic enterprises and support agencies like Local Enterprise Trusts, not very much has been done so far to work out a systematic approach to the redevelopment of local economies and the regeneration of local work. There are one or two local voluntary groups now, for example at Newport and Nevern in Wales, that have come into existence specifically to promote greater local economic self-reliance in energy, by identifying ways in which local work could make a greater contribution to meeting local energy needs; and these are backed by support units set up by such organisations as the Intermediate Technology Development Group (ITDG) and the NCVO. But there is still a lot to be done to provide local areas in general with the kind of guidance they will need to identify ways in which local work could be used to meet local needs, and thus to clarify the context in which new local enterprises are likely to find a successful role.

Business and Industry

Those who direct and manage business and industry do not yet, on the whole, share the perspective of this book – that a shift of historic significance has already begun that will take us from the age of employment into the age of ownwork. There are a few business leaders who have publicly recognised that conventional full employment will not return, and who have lent their authority to programmes of research and consultation on the consequences of this. But, by and large, most businesspeople and industrialists do not have a vision of a future in which people will work for themselves.

Nonetheless, the actions of business and industry in recent years have encouraged the shift towards ownwork in a number of ways.

There has been the straightforward matter of developing a market for the new small-scale technologies and equipments, and DIY materials and products of all kinds that are already helping to revive economic activity in small concerns at the local level, and to expand informal productive activity in the household. Home-brewing and home-computing are two examples among many that have come to the fore in recent years. But, in general, there have been important developments of this kind in : food-growing and food-processing; health monitoring and maintenance; energy for heating, light and power; waste-disposal and recycling; clothing; building, carpentry, plumbing, electrics, and interior decorating; and repair, maintenance and servicing of all kinds. A recent series of reports identified brewing, printing, brick-making, wool textiles, plastics and other recycling industries, and garage repairs and servicing, as types of business which new small-scale technologies and equipments now make economically possible to run on a small, local scale.[3] For the future, the scope for businesses to develop this market for small-scale equipments and easy-to-use materials is very great.

Then there is the employment role of business and industry. As employers, many large businesses have taken steps in recent years which have contributed to the shift towards ownwork. For example, there is the growing trend for professional employees and salespeople to work from their own homes instead of the company office, relying on the telephone and (increasingly) the computer to keep them in touch. There is also the trend for large companies to hive off activities previously carried out by employees, such as catering, cleaning, printing, or gardening, by converting employees to independent workers under contract. There are many cases of large companies, such as Dunlop or ICI, making new arrangements of this kind by setting their former employees up in business to work on their own account and giving them a guaranteed contract of work for an initial period of time. Perhaps the best publicised example of this kind of thing in Britain has been the Rank Xerox scheme, under which a number of senior Rank Xerox staff were converted from being full-time employees to being independent free-lance consultants, given a part-time contract with the company to continue working for it for a specified period, set up in good new office accommodation of their own, and encouraged to develop additional business with other clients. The saving in office space and the other overheads that go with employing senior staff was said to be one of the main reasons why Rank Xerox decided to make this change.

Further examples of the trend towards ownwork in the organisation of big company work are to be found in the general tendency towards decentralisation that is now evident. In both Sweden and the United States the terms 'intrapreneur' and 'intrapreneurship' have been used in recent years to refer to the development of entrepreneurial ways of working within large companies. A more fashionable term for the same thing is 'skunkworks'. This seems to have more appeal than 'intrapreneur' to the transatlantic business mind.

Some employers have also begun to accept more flexible conditions of work for their employees, which reduce the amount of time they work in their job and give them more time for work of their own, such as looking after their families. Already a shift is beginning to be apparent towards more part-time jobs, including job-sharing, and early retirement is increasing. Paternity leave, as well as maternity leave, is becoming customary in some countries, though not in others. Like all changes, the widespread introduction of part-time work will continue to meet some resistance from managements and trade unions, even though increasing numbers of employees will welcome it. But the first steps towards it have already been taken.

More generally, the reduction of the time worked by employees in full-time jobs, that has taken place over the last century or more, has been continuing in recent years. But progress here has been fairly slow. This is becauses employers have insisted that shorter working hours must be accompanied by corresponding improvements in productivity or reductions in pay, while trade unions have insisted that they must not. There are signs in attitude surveys and opinion surveys that some employees, especially but not only in the older age groups, are becoming readier to trade money for time, in other words to accept some reduction in pay for having more time of their own. But it will probably take some significant change in circumstance, such as the introduction of a Guaranteed Basic Income (GBI), to create a substantial breakthrough here.

Another way in which employers have encouraged individual employees to move into ownwork is as a response to redundancy. A number of companies – including such well-known names as ICI, Rank Xerox, Pilkingtons, and Whitbreads – which have been faced with the need to reduce their workforce, including their managerial and professional staff, have resettled redundant managers who opted for it, in self-employed work. In carrying out these changes, a number of companies have found that many of their employees value secure full-time employment less highly than was previously assumed; for example, more employees than expected already have small businesses of their own on the side, and are glad to have the opportunity to put more time into these. As part of the resettlement package, their employer may be able to provide them with various forms of technical and financial advice, with access to investment funds on favourable terms, and – in some cases – with office accommodation and equipment.

Those, then, are some of the ways in which business organisations, as employers, have been helping individual employees to move towards ownwork. They have also been helping to create opportunities for small-scale local employment. In principle, this help has taken two distinct forms. First, a number of large employers like the British Steel Corporation which have had to close major works in particular localities like Corby, thereby creating high levels of local unemployment, have taken direct action to provide facilities and workshop space to enable former employees to set up their own businesses. Second, many large companies have helped to sponsor Local Enterprise Trusts, mentioned earlier in this chapter, with the aim of encouraging new local enterprise and local employment. In practice, the dividing line between these two approaches is blurred. For example, the St. Helens Trust was set up primarily in response to local unemployment created by redundancies at Pilkingtons, the glass company which dominated the town of St. Helens. But it took a form in which other companies, a trade union, one of the big banks, the local authority and the local chamber of commerce all played a part.

By the end of 1984, about 170 Local Enterprise Trusts had been set up in Britain, and more were being formed or were under discussion. The biggest is the London Enterprise Agency. A co-ordinating organisation called Business in the Community was set up in 1981. It is estimated that over 1,000 British companies are now involved in sponsoring Local Enterprise Trusts and similar local enterprise agencies. Many of these companies have seconded managers from among their own staff to set up and run them.

It might be wrong to suggest that business involvement in the shift towards personal and local ownwork in the ways I have briefly outlined has been due to altruism or to any kind of philosophical conviction that the main path of economic development for the future must lead generally in the direction of personal and local self-reliance.[4] Hitherto, at least, business involvement is best understood as simply one aspect of the management of contraction. It is a response to the business problems arising from the need of many big businesses to reduce their workforce and to avoid the public relations damage which this could cause. But, whatever the motivation at this stage, the fact is that what big business has been doing in this respect in the last five years or so, has been an important contribution to the process by which employment in big impersonal organisations is beginning to be replaced by work in small, personal and local units.

Local Government
One of the biggest changes in the last ten years has been the

acceptance of responsibility for the local economy and local employment by local authorities, which were traditionally regarded as responsible mainly for social and environmental services. This has happened in response to the collapse of local economies and local employment, especially in towns and districts which had become dependent on one or more big industries, such as steel or shipbuilding, in which heavy cutbacks have been made in the workforce.

The response of local authorities has taken many forms. At the orthodox end of the spectrum action has been taken to make particular localities more attractive to potential employers, for example by investing in industrial and commercial facilities and by removing existing obstacles to industrial and commercial development. At the other end of the spectrum local authorities have channelled resources directly to particular groups of residents who, because of their deprived circumstances, need special assistance to find work or to survive long periods of unemployment. Many local authorities are now among the sponsors of Local Enterprise Trusts, and have directly provided resources to private employers and voluntary sector groups to organised projects which will attract funding from Manpower Service Commission programmes such as the Youth Training Scheme or the Community Programme. Many have undertaken their own local programmes, for example to restore derelict land and create new parklands (as the Greater Manchester Council have done), and have been able to use Manpower Service Commission money to employ local unemployed people on these programmes. Metropolitan authorities in the West Midlands, Greater London, Merseyside and elsewhere have set up their own Enterprise Boards and Development Corporations to foster new local economic activity and jobs. Some councils, as in South Yorkshire, have begun to use their own employment policies and their own purchasing policies as instruments for encouraging new, more flexible patterns of employment and local work to produce goods and services that are locally needed.

It is true that much of the response by local authorities, as by business and industry, to the unemployment crisis has been aimed at the creation of conventional jobs or at providing palliatives for people who are unemployed. It is also generally true that local government is at present too centralised and too remote from the communities in which people actually live and work. Nonetheless, the very fact that local responsibility for employment and other aspects of the local economy is now accepted can be seen as a pointer in the direction of ownwork. Real progress will not be made until increasing numbers of local residents and local workers begin to take more direct control over the self-management of local housing, local neighbourhood services, and local productive activities. But the encouragement already given by some local authorities to community housing associations, community enterprises and local co-operatives already points in this direction. Two relevant recent initiatives by new town development corporations are the Lightmoor project at Telford and the Greentown project at Milton Keynes, where potential residents of new communities have been encouraged to come together in advance, so that they themselves can plan and develop the community they will live in.

Central Government and International Government Agencies
In so far as central governments and international agencies like the EEC and OECD have directly concerned themselves with work and employment, the main aim of their policies has been to create new jobs. Many different kinds of incentives have been given to employers and potential employers to invest in new plant and equipment, especially in selected regions and enterprise zones, and to provide jobs or training places for the long-term unemployed and the young unemployed. These policies have not, in general, been very successful. They have been costly. Their main effects have been to accelerate the replacement of existing jobs in some firms by the creation of new jobs in others, and the replacement of existing jobs in unselected regions and zones by the creation of new jobs in selected regions or zones; and to give new jobs to people who qualify under the schemes instead of people who do not.

Some of the measures that have been introduced to provide work and training for unemployed people, and especially the young unemployed and the long-term unemployed, have however pointed broadly in the direction of ownwork. They may, in the course of time, turn out to have provided

stepping-stones to it. I am referring particularly to some of the
Manpower Service Commission schemes in Britain. One of
these is the Enterprise Allowance Scheme already mentioned,
which helps unemployed people to start up in business on
their own. The Community Programme is another. It provides funds for projects that are of benefit to the community,
and makes it possible for 'managing agencies' representing
community interests to provide work for groups of unemployed people. In many cases it should eventually be possible
to build up those groups of workers to the point where they
become viable as small co-operatives or community enterprises. The main difficulty so far has been that these schemes
have been designed as short-term palliatives. The length of
time that unemployed people may stay on them is strictly
limited and they are hedged about with constraints intended
to prevent people working on them from competing for work
with unionised labour employed in conventional jobs. This
has limited the ability of local groups operating the schemes to
use them to launch local people in sustainable enterprises of
their own.

But, as time has passed and the unemployment crisis has
grown worse, the value and the potential of unconventional
local employment initiatives of this kind have been more fully
appreciated and understood. In particular, both the EEC and
the OECD have launched major programmes in the last two or
three years, to study the part played by local employment
initiatives, and to give guidelines to member countries on how
to encourage them.

Other Institutions

Among those who have begun to be concerned about the
future of work, and about the change that will be necessary in
their own role and function if full employment is not going to
return, are some leading trade unionists, a growing number of
teachers and others in the educational profession, and a certain number of planners.

As we have seen in Chapter 8, Clive Jenkins and Barrie Sherman are two leading trade unionists who argue that the
'collapse of work' must be faced and that trade unions must
prepare to meet the 'leisure shock'. It is true that the trade
union movement as a whole has not yet begun to recognise

that something of this kind may be happening. Its main energies in the last few years have been channelled into what it still sees as the fight for jobs. After all, the trade unions originally came into existence to represent the interests of employed people. Their main goals have been to preserve employment, and to improve the pay and conditions attaching to it. They have never campaigned for part-time employment for people who wanted it. Nor have they concerned themselves directly with the interests of people not in employment. It has certainly never been their aim to enable people to undertake useful and rewarding work outside employment. Indeed, they have understandably seen all forms of ownwork as open to exploitation by unscrupulous employers and therefore as a threat to their own members. But, although there is little sign in the activities of the trade unions so far that the shift to ownwork is now under way, the new thinking has at least begun.

Rightly or wrongly, the assumption on which many teachers used to operate was that, if pupils and students did reasonably well, they had a good chance of getting a decent job. Teachers were able to tell their pupils correctly that if they worked hard at their studies they would be rewarded that way. Now that is no longer the case. What are teachers to do about it? Many are beginning to recognise that the problem goes very deep. If full employment has gone for ever, what does this imply for the curriculum? What should pupils and students learn, to prepare them for a life in which there may be no jobs for them? And how and where should they learn? Teachers and educationalists like Philip Toogood and Tony Watts[5] are facing up to these questions. There is a chance that some of the training which will be funded under the Youth Training Scheme by the Manpower Services Commission will prove relevant for life without employment. And there has been some public discussion about the possible desirability of extending schemes like Community Service Volunteers, which enable young people to learn from the experience of community service.[6] So, even if on the whole it cannot yet be said that the education profession has seriously begun to come to terms with the prospect of the transition from employment to ownwork, the ground for this has now begun to be prepared.

So far as the planning profession is concerned, there is growing unease in the profession about the unsuitability of most of the houses provided under public housing programmes for the more economical and self-reliant lifestyles that many people will have to adopt if full employment does not return. Most of these houses are expensive on energy and maintenance costs, and provide no facilities for people to do any work for themselves, paid or unpaid, in and around their home. The lay-out of recently-planned towns, based on the assumption that most people will go to an employer's premises in an industrial zone to work, and will have access to convenient transport to take them from their residential zone to do their shopping, to take their children to and from school, to get to the hospital, and so on, is also a cause for concern in the profession. The Town and Country Planning Association has been playing a prominent part in articulating these concerns and – for example, by promoting the Greentown and Lightmoor projects mentioned above – in helping to prepare the way for the development of more self-reliant, self-managed communities and for the enabling role which this will require of the planning profession.[7]

It is still possible, for people who see things that way, to argue that the recent developments outlined in this chapter do not necessarily show that a significant change has begun to take place in the dominant pattern of work. It is not yet possible to convince them that the recent rise in personal and local ownwork will, in the long run, amount to more than a marginal alternative to conventional employment. But, at the same time, those who do believe in the possibility of a shift away from dependent employment to more self-reliant ownwork, can interpret much that has started to happen in the last few years as the first halting steps in that direction.[8]

The Ownwork Agenda

In this chapter we look at some of the changes that will have to be made in order to facilitate the further expansion of personal and local ownwork. They include changes in how people get their money incomes; easier personal access to the workspace, land and capital needed for ownwork; the development of the personal skills needed for ownwork, including the ability to organise the use of one's own money, time and space; and changes needed to facilitate more self-reliant local economic development, including the investment of local resources and local money in local work to meet local needs.

Personal Incomes
We have touched already, in Chapters 4 and 9, on the need to loosen the link between money incomes and paid employment. As citizens of late industrial societies, we already accept that all citizens should receive a basic subsistence income, and we accept collective responsibility for providing such an income to our fellow-citizens who cannot provide one for themselves. But we still make the assumption that the proper and normal thing is for people to earn a sufficient income for themselves and their dependants out of paid employment. This assumption is based on other assumptions which are now no longer valid – for example: that almost all paid jobs will provide an adequate subsistence income; that full-time formal employment from 16 to 65 will remain the norm, at least for men; that married women can continue to be treated as financial dependants of their husbands; and that people who cannot support themselves and their dependants by their earnings from paid employment will be so few as to be an easily manageable exception to the general rule.[1]
This means that those who cannot provide themselves with

165

enough income from work, either because they are unemployed or because they are low paid, are treated as second-
class citizens who have failed to meet the norm. They have to
register and submit themselves to bureaucratic scrutiny and
approval in order to receive unemployment and social
security benefits; this often involves harassment and snooping
into their private lives. The administration of these benefits
requires an expensive and complex bureaucracy. Their
receipt is subject to conditions which severely limit the
recipients' freedom to commit themselves to useful activities,
including training and voluntary work (since they must keep
themselves 'available' to take up a paid job, if one should offer
itself), and which prevent them from trying to build up paid
work on their own account. The assumption is that a conventional job is still the norm, and that people who don't have a
job can do no work.

This present method of guaranteeing a basic income for all
is clearly now out of date, in the light of the high unemployment levels that are in prospect for the next 10 or 15 years, and
– to put it no higher – the possibility that conventional full
employment will never be restored. At the very least, the conditions governing the receipt of benefits must be relaxed so
that people receiving them are enabled to spend their time
usefully, and to build up new ways of earning an income for
themselves. The Enterprise Allowance Scheme mentioned in
the last chapter is one small example of this. Such arrangements for liberating people from the 'poverty trap' will have to
be extended.

However, simply to relax the existing conditions on which
benefits are received will, in fact, do no more than tinker with
the problem. The real problem is the false perception of the
realities of work and incomes in late industrial society as it has
developed over the last 40 years. The time has come to disen-
tangle the obligation to provide all citizens with an adequate
basic income from the out-of-date prescription that the normal way for most people to get such an income must be to
earn it in a job. In other words, it is time to introduce an
unconditional Guaranteed Basic Income (GBI) under which all
citizens, rich and poor, men and women, old and young, will
automatically receive a weekly basic income from the state.

Increasingly serious discussion of this idea has been taking place in a number of countries in recent years.[2] In Britain, a proposed scheme has been considered by a Select Committee of Parliament, and a Working Party to explore the practical possibilities has been set up by the National Council for Voluntary Organisations (NCVO). Broadly speaking, what is proposed is a consolidation of personal income tax and personal benefits, allowances and grants on the following lines:[3]

(1) All citizens will be paid a weekly personal basic income into their bank or giro account, geared to a minimum living standard. Special rates will apply to children, pensioners and the disabled. This unconditional basic income will replace most existing benefits, grants and tax allowances. It will not be taxable.

(2) All citizens will be free to undertake paid work to add to their basic income. All income over and above the basic income will be taxed.

(3) Receipts from the tax on incomes, plus savings from the abolition of existing tax allowances, grants and benefits, and from the reduction in the cost of administering them, together perhaps with some increase in expenditure taxes such as Value Added Tax (VAT), will finance the basic income.

The underlying principle of such a scheme is simple. The precise details of how it would work and how it would be funded are complex. I do not propose to go into these here. Detailed discussion of the various options will be found in the publications referred to in Note (2) to this chapter. But some further discussion of the arguments for and against a GBI is necessary.

The arguments for it include the following:

(1) Citizens will no longer be divided into two classes: those in well-paid employment, and those who have to apply for state benefits because they are unemployed or in low-paid jobs. Everyone will receive their basic income equally as of right. The GBI will thus have a socially equalising effect.

(2) The poverty trap will automatically be abolished. No one who earns money for themselves will have their benefits withdrawn and incur a liability to tax in such a way that, as

happens often now, they are left worse off than they were before. The incentive for poorer people to find useful work and to better their own situation by their own efforts will be much improved.

(3) This means that much activity of the kind we now call the black economy, involving the concealment of earnings so that benefits may continue to be received, will be legitimised. People who are in receipt of their basic income from the state will no longer be forbidden to add to it by taking on paid work.

(4) Greater equality will be created between men and women. In fact, one way of thinking of the basic income is as wages for housework for all citizens. The basic income will make it easier for men, as well as for women, to spend more time on the informal work of looking after the home and the family; and to choose whether or not to seek paid employment outside the home. It will make it easier for men and women alike, regardless of their age, to look for part-time paid work which leaves them free for part-time unpaid work in the home and the family.

(5) It will become easier for many more people than today to spend some of their time on local activities of a voluntary or semi-voluntary nature, and thus to contribute directly to the welfare and amenity of themselves, their families and their fellow-citizens, and reduce the dependence of people in their locality generally on the services of the welfare state.

(6) Finally, in addition to all these primarily social advantages, the GBI will have economic advantages from the point of view of employers, workers, and the community as a whole. It will make it possible to re-establish a free market in labour. Employers will no longer be responsible for paying their employees' basic income and will therefore be free to pay them as much or as little as they think they can afford. Employees, on the other hand, will already be receiving their basic income from the state, and will be free to accept as much or as little pay as they may decide. Employers and employees will both be freed from many of the constraints imposed by the present employment relationship. The GBI will thus have an economically liberating effect all round. On the one hand, it will reduce the wages and salaries paid for many kinds of work, and by excluding the basic subsistence element in workers' incomes from employers' costs on wages and salaries, it will encourage economic competitiveness. On the other

hand, by reducing the present degree of dependence of poorer workers on unpleasant, menial work, it will probably make it necessary to increase the wages now paid for doing such work. Both these effects will be welcome.

To sum up the arguments in favour, the GBI will lead to a liberation of work, helping to remove the existing divisions between people who are employed and people who are unemployed, between people of working age and people who are retired, and between men's work and women's work. In place of these divisions it will open up a wide range of equally valid work options for all, including: no paid work but plenty of informal, voluntary work and productive leisure; irregular paid work; a regular part-time job; a full-time job; and even, for some eager spirits, more than one full-time job. As well as providing all citizens with a basic income without loss of dignity, it will create opportunities for rewarding work in the formal and informal economy alike, it will contribute to greater economic efficiency, and it will enable much necessary work to be done that cannot be economically done at all so long as conventional employment continues to be treated as the norm.

On the other side of the account, the following are the main arguments brought against the GBI:

(1) If the basic income paid to every citizen is high enough for the poorest and least capable to live on, the rates of tax needed to finance it will be too high. For example, it has been calculated that if all the money required for distribution as basic income were raised from taxes on personal incomes, a uniform tax rate of 50% on all personal incomes above the basic income level would have to be brought in. On the other hand, if all the money were raised by VAT, a VAT rate of 100% would have to be imposed. In the first case, it is argued, the 50% income tax would discourage people from taking paid work. In the second, a VAT rate of 100% would be much too regressive, bearing very heavily on the poor in comparison with the rich.

(2) People's personal circumstances vary so widely that the level of an adequate subsistence income is correspondingly bound to vary widely between different people. To take two extreme examples, people who own their own houses outright, who have gardens in which they can grow their own

food, and who live in the country where they can supplement their diet from the fields and hedgerows, pick up firewood in the woods, and enjoy inexpensive outdoor leisure pursuits, will need a lower basic income than people who live in rented energy-expensive flats in tower blocks in city centres. It would be unfair if the state were to pay the same basic income to people in such different circumstances as these. An adequate income for people in the the first category would be inadequate for those in the second, whereas an adequate income for the latter would be unnecessarily high for the former.

These arguments cannot be ignored. But closer examination shows them to be less conclusive than might appear at first sight.

Against the first of the arguments, the most important thing to point out is that there cannot be any fundamental problem about finding the money to pay everyone a basic income, because everyone receives a basic income already. The GBI would merely change the mechanics for doing this. It would provide an administratively simpler and cheaper way of achieving what is already done – that is, guaranteeing everyone a basic income and taxing what they receive over and above it.

What the first argument is actually saying is that many people, on receiving an unconditional basic income from the state, will be unwilling to continue working to top up the basic income, and will relax into featherbedded idleness. But what most people actually do now, whether they are among those receiving benefits from the state or among those who earn their income from paid employment, provides no evidence in support of this. On the contrary, most people today – whether they are employed or not – want an income higher than the basic subsistence level; they work for it if they can, openly if they are in employment, in the black economy if they are receiving benefits. On balance, it is much more likely that the introduction of a GBI will result in people looking for and finding paid work who are not allowed to do so today, than in people deciding to drop out of paid work who are in it now.

In practice, what happens will depend to a certain extent on the levels set for the basic income and the taxes needed to finance it. The higher the basic income and the higher the level of personal tax, the greater the disincentive to take on paid work. Setting these levels will become a central political issue, with a general tendency for those on the right to favour low levels with a lower redistribution of incomes from the rich to the poor, and for those on the left to favour higher levels with a higher redistributive effect.

So far as the suggested rates of a 50% tax on personal incomes or 100% VAT are concerned, the picture is not so daunting as might be supposed at first sight. Keith Roberts[2] has estimated that businesses will be paying wages, salaries and other costs at about half their present level (because the cost of the basic income of everyone in paid work will no longer be included in their wages and salaries), and that prices of goods and services in the shops (before VAT) will therefore be about half their present level. If that is correct, a 50% tax on earned incomes would mean that the actual purchasing power of what a paid worker receives will be more or less the same as it would have been if prices had been twice as high and if there had been no tax on income. Similarly, a 100% rate of VAT would restore the actual prices paid by purchasers for goods and services to more or less what they would have been as matters are arranged today.

But, of course, the 50% tax on personal incomes and a 100% rate of VAT are just figures that have been brought into the discussion for illustrative purposes, to indicate broadly the scale on which money will have to be raised to finance a GBI. In practice, basic incomes will probably be funded, at least initially, by combining a progressive tax on incomes above the basic level with a rate of VAT lower than 100%. For practical purposes this seems the most sensible basis on which preparations should now be made for phasing in the introduction of the GBI, perhaps over a ten-year transition period.[4]

However, at least two other potential new sources of some of the money needed to pay basic incomes may be available, to be brought in as partial substitutes for personal income tax and VAT in due course. The first is to do with the way new purchasing power is created. The second is a tax on land.

The fact that new purchasing power is continually being created and injected into the economy is not in dispute. New money and credit is now created by the banks lending money to their customers, including the government; the customers then either deposit this money in the banking system or pay it to other people who deposit it there; in either case the supply of money deposited with the banks has been increased. As an aspect of monetary policy governments can exercise some control over the amount of new credit created by the banks and thus over the amount by which the money supply is increased. But this control is fairly hit-or-miss. Moreover, why should increases in the money supply be channelled, according to criteria which the banks decide, in the form of loans to a selected category of people (and organisations), namely credit-worthy bank customers who want to borrow money? Might it not be better from every point of view, except for the effect on bank profits, if whatever increase in the money supply is thought to be desirable from time to time were created directly by the government, and injected into the economy in the first instance in the form of an equal distribution to all citizens as part of their basic income?

This proposal is related to the ideas put forward by C.H. Douglas and the Social Credit movement after the First World War.[5] They have always been succcessfully resisted by the banks, however, and it therefore may not be realistic to look forward to the introduction of anything on these lines until the banking system itself faces a serious possibility of collapse – which may not be many years away (see Chapter 9). The time has certainly come to dust off the idea that the distribution of new money and credit regularly to all citizens by the state might be a better way to create new money and credit than the way it is done today, and to examine its practical details. It could be a relevant response to the weakening of the link between work and money incomes, and the transition from employment to ownwork.

So far as land taxation is concerned, no figure is available for the total unimproved annual rental value of all the land in Britain. But clearly, if that sum were distributed annually in equal parts to all citizens, it too would make a useful contribution to the financing of the annual basic income. However, there are other important arguments in favour of land taxation, and it will be more appropriate to discuss it in the next section of this chapter.

To conclude our discussion of personal incomes, the introduction of the GBI will be a historical milestone of the first importance. By officially disconnecting subsistence from paid employment it will mark the transition to the post-employment age, as surely as the repeal of the Corn Laws in 1846 marked the transition from an agricultural to an industrial society. It will start reversing the process that began several hundred years ago, when the common people were deprived of access to land and the wherewithal to provide their own subsistence, and so became dependent on paid labour.

Access to Workspace, Land and Capital
As we saw in Chapter 4, the houses and the cities, towns and villages in which we live today have taken shape around the assumption that most people will be working for employers. Architects have designed houses, especially houses provided by the public sector for people in the less well-off section of society, to be places of consumption and leisure, not to be places of work and production. Planners have divided cities, towns and villages into zones, imposing a physical separation on the activities of living, working, shopping, and so on. Few people have had access to land for productive purposes on their own account. The assumption has been that employers will own and provide the land and buildings where people work. The prices of land in most industrialised countries are now so high that few people can afford to buy it and work on it for themselves. Another assumption has been that most people will not need the capital necessary to support their work and that employers will supply it. So, while redistribution of income has always been high on the agenda for progressive politicians, the possibilities for redistributing capital have not. Even institutional changes such as the conversion of commercial firms into a co-operative form and the wider spread of share ownership have received lukewarm attention; and, of course, the nationalisation of railways, coalmining, electricity, broadcasting, and so on, has never meant nor been intended to mean the kind of redistribution of capital which would enable more people to finance their own work and provide themselves with their own means of production.

The transition from the age of employment to the age of ownwork will require big changes in all these respects.

Architects and planners will increasingly have to recognise

that a post-employment society will use physical space in distinctly different ways from a society organised around employment, and that these new patterns of use will imply a distinctly different approach to both architecture and planning than the one that has been dominant in the last half century or more. There will be exciting new opportunities here for those architects and planners who can grasp them. One expanding role for their professions will be to enable increasing numbers of people not in full-time employment to design and build (or part-build)their own homes, and – as in the Greentown and Lightmoor projects mentioned in Chapter 11 – to plan and build (or part-build) their own communities.

So far as access to land is concerned, we saw in Chapter 9 that a decline in the capital values of land and property would be likely to follow any significant decline in the cash flows – and expectation of future cash flows – on which existing values depend. In the case of agricultural land, such a decline in value would follow a reduction in the level of financial support for agriculture provided at present by national and international policies such as the Common Agricultural Policy (CAP) of the European Community. It would also be caused by a shift to less intensive agricultural practices, either for economic reasons because of the rising costs of fuel, fertilisers, pesticides and anti-pollution safeguards, or for physical reasons owing to the deterioration of soils subjected to intensive farming methods over the long term.[6]

Any such decline in agricultural and, for that matter, urban land values will tend to make it easier to find land on which to work and live for individuals and groups of people without large sums of existing capital. But more positive measures will have to be introduced as well. They may include land taxation. They will certainly include new forms of land tenure and new procedures for acquiring land by people with no existing capital and no regular income or other security on which to borrow.

The best-known advocate of land taxation has been Henry George. In *Progress and Poverty*,[7] first published in 1879, he argued strongly for the taxation of land, to replace other taxes:

> To shift the burden of taxation from production and exchange to the value or rent of land would be not merely to give new

stimulus to the production of wealth; it would be to open new opportunities. For under this system no one would care to hold land unless to use it, and land now withheld from use would everywhere be thrown open to improvement. And it must be remembered that this would apply not merely to agricultural land but to all land. Mineral land would be thrown open to use as would agricultural land; and in the heart of a city no one could afford to keep land from its most profitable use, or on the outskirts to demand more for it than would be warranted by the use to which it could be put at the time.

Whoever planted an orchard, or sowed a field, or built a house, or erected a manufactory, no matter how costly, would have no more to pay in taxes than if he kept so much land idle. The owner of a vacant city lot would have to pay as much for the privilege of keeping other people off it until he wanted to use it as his neighbour who has a fine house upon his lot. It would cost as much to keep a row of tumble-down shanties upon valuable land as it would were the land covered with a grand hotel or a pile of great warehouses filled with costly goods.

The selling price of land would fall; land speculation would receive its death-blow; land monopolisation would no longer pay. Thus there would disappear the premium which, wherever labour is most productive, must now be paid before labour can be exerted. The farmer would not have to pay out half his means, or mortgage his labour for years, in order to obtain land to cultivate. The company that proposed to erect a manufactory would not have to expend a great part of its capital for a site.

Henry George, like Adam Smith 100 years before – see Chapter 7 – assumed that all economic activity was limited to the formal economy, and that all economic agents fell into the three categories of landholder, capitalist or labourer, receiving money returns in the form of rent, profit (and interest), and wages for their respective contributions to the economic process. He also assumed that, if land were taxed, all other taxes could be removed. He thus defended land taxation against its opponents on the following grounds:

When it is first proposed to put all taxes upon the value of land and thus to confiscate rent, there will not be wanting appeals to the fears of small farm and homestead owners, who will be told that this is a proposition to rob them of their hard-earned property. But a moment's reflection will show that this proposition should commend itself to all whose interests as landholders do not largely exceed their interests as labourers or capitalists, or both.

Take the case of the mechanic, shopkeeper or professional man who has secured himself a house and plot where he lives and which he contemplates with satisfaction as a place from which his family cannot be ejected in case of his death. Although he will have taxes to pay upon his land, he will be released from taxes upon his house and improvements, upon his furniture and personal property, upon all that he and his family eat, drink and wear, while his earnings will be largely increased by the rise of wages, the constant employment, and the increased briskness of trade.

And so with the farmer. I speak not of the farmer who never touches the handles of a plough, but of the working farmer who holds a small farm which he cultivates with the aid of his sons and perhaps some hired help. He would be a great gainer by the substitution of a single tax upon the value of land for all the taxes now imposed on commodities because the taxation of land values rests only on the value of land, which is low in agricultural districts as compared with towns and cities, where it is high. Acre for acre, the improved and cultivated farm with its buildings, fences, orchard, crops and stock, would be taxed no more than unused land of equal quality. For taxes, being levied upon the value of the land alone, would fall with equal incidence upon unimproved as upon improved land.

George's most important arguments in favour of land taxation are valid for us today. It will bring down the price of land. It will make land more accessible for those who want to use it. It will encourage the use of land, as opposed to its retention unused in the hope that its capital value will appreciate. It will also ensure that increases in the value of unimproved land, which arise out of the activities of the community around it, accrue to the community and not to the owner who has done nothing to create the increase in value. But our context today differs from George's in two important respects. First, it would be unreasonable for us 100 years later than George to expect that land taxation will altogether replace other taxes. Second, we are concerned not only, as he was, to liberate formal work i.e. work that brings in a money return and contributes to conventionally measured economic growth. We are concerned also to open up new opportunities for informal work, and to revive the informal economy. To be more specific, our concern is that people should be enabled to occupy and use land, not only for money-earning work, but also for work and activities that contribute to their own needs and the needs of others, without necessarily bringing in a money income or at least without bringing in the full commercial return that might be attainable from their piece of land. A question that must be asked therefore is whether, when a GBI and a land tax have both been introduced, people who earn no additional income but who live and work informally on their own piece of land should be liable to pay land tax. In principle, the answer should be Yes. In practice, this will have to be examined as part of the detailed study of the precise forms and levels both of basic income and of land taxation that will be needed in response to the decline of employment.

New forms of land tenure and land purchase which enable people without capital of their own to have access to land are already being developed, though on a small scale as yet. Land trusts, community land trusts, community development trusts and community land banks are among the structures now being set up in Britain and North America for this purpose.[8] Even from existing financial institutions, these trusts can often raise finance, for purchase and development of land, against the security of the land itself. However, the end of the employment age will require the development of new channels of investment in small-scale local activities generally, to provide the capital they need, not only for land acquisition but for other purposes too.

Local Economic Development
Three particular items come on to the ownwork agenda under this heading. The first is a cultivation of awareness in the minds of people that their local economy belongs to them as participants in it. The second is systematic analysis of the ways in which local economies can be strengthened. The third is the development of local economic institutional structures.

Many people today are hardly aware of being participants in the local economy; they work elsewhere and invest their savings elsewhere; many even do their shopping elsewhere, in hypermarkets and supermarkets that stock no local products.

Many who *are* conscious of being participants in the local economy perceive themselves as passively dependent on local economic events outside their own control. Many people perceive local economic life as almost wholly dependent on national and international policies and contingencies over which they have no influence at all. I noticed recently in discussions about the future of work, how little aware many metropolitan councillors (elected representatives) seemed to be that the inhabitants of their big conurbation might have scope to meet local needs through local work. The councillors were more concerned to criticise the national government for its policies, than to respond with constructive local action. A top priority is to help people in every walk of life to become aware of themselves as participants in the local economy, of the extent to which they can expand it or diminish it by their own economic behaviour, and of all the various ways in which they could – if they so decided – help to make it more flourishing.

The second item stems directly from this. Virtually no systematic analysis has yet been done of the various measures which local people might take in the mid-1980s, in order to meet a greater proportion of local needs with local work. Such analysis is urgently necessary. It should cover all the most important needs of local people – for food, energy, housing, clothing, other goods of all kinds, commercial services and social services. [9] Ideally, it may be found, analyses of this kind will be needed for localities of three different population sizes: up to, say, five thousand; up to, say, a hundred thousand; and up to, say, two million. But these figures should be taken as no more than an indication of the general nature of what is required. Without at this stage pre-supposing that existing local boundaries will provide the most practical basis for the move towards greater local economic self-sufficiency, we need to examine the possible ways in which local people can try to achieve it at what we now broadly think of as parish, district and conurbation levels.

Local authorities, local enterprise trusts, and local universities, polytechnics and other centres of higher education and research should themselves carry out such studies, and provide resources, help and advice to local groups who want to do the same. At the national level, bodies like the Institute of Local Government and the Centre for Urban and Regional Studies (both attached to Birmingham University), and the School for Advanced Urban Studies (attached to Bristol University), research bodies such as the Policy Studies Institute, university faculties of economics, and consultancy organisations specialising in the subject of work and economic development, should be encouraged to clarify the practical implications of adopting self-reliance as a main principle of local economic development. They should aim to offer generally applicable guidance and help, and to suggest a systematic approach, to local authorities and local groups wishing to explore the specific possibilities for their own local area.

New local economic institutions will be needed to reflect and to facilitate the transition from local dependence on externally organised employment to local reliance on locally directed ownwork. Local enterprise trusts and unemployment centres will no doubt prove to be among the forerunners of these new institutions, as may be the new departments in local government authorities that have been set up to deal with local unemployment and economic problems. The development of community enterprises and co-operatives, and community development agencies, on a widening scale will call for banking and credit institutions to support them. These may include new institutions, such as co-operative land banks, local credit unions, and local investment trusts, as well as decentralised adaptations of today's centralised banking and financial institutions. Even the possibility of developing local currencies as a strand in local economic revival should not be ignored.

The actual process of developing the required new institutional structures can be foreseeen as an iterative process. A variety of practical local responses to specific local needs will provide material for more general analyses of such local experiences, and for more systematic studies of the functions that new local economic institutions should undertake. In turn, these general and systematic studies will provide information and help to local people, enabling them to set up more effective arrangements specific to the development needs of their own localities.

Technology

The demand for small-scale technologies will continue to grow and market forces will increasingly push scientists, engineers and industrialists into inventions, innovations and product developments which will meet this growing demand. Those who fail to establish themselves in the expanding new fields of technology which support personal and local ownwork, will be overtaken by their competitors.

A useful criterion, which business strategists can use to judge whether a new technological development is consistent with the ownwork agenda, is to ask whether the new material, or equipment, or process, or system is likely to enlarge the range of competence, control and initiative of the people who will be affected by it; or whether it is more likely to subordinate them to more powerful people and organisations, and make them dependent on bureaucracies and machines which they cannot themselves control.

But it is not only business strategists, scientists and engineers who will be involved in this approach. Government agencies and universities will have a role too. For, as long as the assumption remains at all widely accepted that it is for organisations – and for large organisations at that – to provide the technology to support people's work and not for people to provide it for themselves, the power to purchase and therefore to specify new technologies will tend to remain centralised in large organisations. This means that there will continue to be a tendency to retard the development of new small-scale technologies. To illustrate this with an obvious example from the immediate past, infinitely more resources have been channelled into the development of nuclear power, a technology which makes the whole population depend for energy supplies on the employees of large centralised organisations, than into the development of domestic heat-pumps or local combined-heat-and-power (CHP) systems, which enable people in their own households and localities to contribute to their own energy needs.

The inertia of the status quo thus tends to retard the development of new small-scale technologies. This creates an artificial time-lag which, if not corrected, will delay unnecessarily the successful introduction of the more decentralised working patterns and lifestyles which will help to solve the crisis of unemployment. This means that government research and development (R and D) has an important part of its own to play in the ownwork agenda.

What is needed first is a systematic survey of fields such as agriculture and food, energy, transport, industrial manufacturing, recycling, repair and maintenance, housing, health, education, information and communication, to establish what existing or new small-scale technologies could be further developed, which will expand the opportunities for personal and local ownwork in those fields.[10] Then, until commercially financed research is willing to take up the projects identified in this way, government R and D establishments and publicly funded contractors should be asked to take them forward. In time, of course, as the shift from employment to ownwork gathers increasing momentum, the emphasis may be expected to shift from large to small new technologies in commercial R and D as well as in R and D which is publicly funded.

It will be seen that the ownwork agenda for technology goes beyond technology assessment, as technology assessment has normally been understood and practised hitherto. The concern underlying technology assessment has generally been a negative concern. The intention has been to avoid the social and environmental side-effects which might be harmful, dangerous or otherwise undesirable, of technologies which businesses or governments proposed to introduce for other reasons. Environmental impact assessments and social impact assessments have been among the techniques most commonly used. The ownwork agenda requires a more positive approach, involving the systematic identification of technological gaps and of new technologies or new uses of existing technologies that will fill them. In other words, it involves the development and use of technologies that are positively benign, in the sense of meeting needs not already met, not just the avoidance and prohibition of technologies that have undesired effects. There is a parallel to this in the field of financial investment. The phrase 'ethical investment' has hitherto tended to be negatively used to refer to the avoidance of investment in countries and businesses considered undesirable, such as South Africa, the arms trade, drugs, alcohol and tobacco. But new ethical investment funds now being set up aim to fill a hitherto unmet need, by giving positive opportunities for investment in businesses and in projects which investors actively wish to support, such as small local businesses or solar energy projects.[11]

It is no doubt unrealistic to hope that governments will put in hand the kind of systematic survey of technological needs that I have mentioned, at least for a year or two longer, until the shift from employment to ownwork has become almost universally accepted. Until that time, a top priority will be for alternative technology and research groups[12] to continue with their work, and for activist groups in the agriculture, energy, transport and other fields to continue to press for resources to be switched away from big technologies to small.

Education, Training, Leisure

The ownwork agenda requires a shift of emphasis in education, training and leisure, so that all these will involve practical skills, self-directed activities, and participation in activities of the local community, to a greater extent than at present. The shift from employment to ownwork will also mean that the distinctions between education and work, training and work, and leisure and work, become less sharp. More education and training will take place than today in the context of work; and people will often find it difficult to say whether they regard some particular activity as work or leisure or a mixture of the two. In these ways learning and leisure will both contribute to satisfying and rewarding ways of living that are more self-reliant, less dependent on employment, and more fully integrated in their local communities, than many people's lives today.

By practical skills I do not mean only the capacity to use small-scale technologies, e.g. for plumbing, electrical work, food-growing, cooking, computing or any other of the hundred and one different technical activities that ownwork may involve. Learning to use a range of these technologies will, indeed, be an important aspect of education and training for ownwork in the post-employment age. By practical skills I also refer to less technical capabilities, like self-confidence and initiative and other personal and interpersonal skills which will rate higher in a life of co-operative self-reliance than in a life based on employment. There are, for example, skills in the use of time, space, and money, which the employee culture of late industrial society has largely been able to ignore. In an employment-based society most people, as employees, have had no need to acquire the habits and skills of planning and organising their own space and time at work, nor of planning and managing cash-flows and financial outlays in connection with their work. Their employer has done all this for them. However, as the shift to ownwork gathers pace, it may be skills like these, even more than specific practical skills of a technical kind, that will prove most necessary and, perhaps, for many people the most difficult to pick up. And there can be no doubt that many existing schools and many existing members of the teaching profession will find them difficult to handle.

What will eventually be needed here, in education, training and leisure, as in other fields, will be a systematic analysis of the changes both in content and context which the shift to ownwork implies, and a systematic reorientation to ownwork of much of what is now provided by way of education, training and leisure for an employment-based society. But again, given that the professions and organisations most deeply involved are rooted in the status quo, it is probably not realistic to expect this to happen until the shift to ownwork is further advanced.

Meanwhile, it will be a top priority for alternative centres[13] of education and training and leisure activity, for such local bodies as Unemployment Centres and Local Enterprise Trusts, and even for official bodies like the Manpower Services Commission which, being more recently established, are less deeply rooted in the old approach, to press ahead with the development of education, training and leisure facilities appropriate to the post-employment age.

Economics, Social Sciences, Management Sciences
Economics and other social sciences, including management sciences, are based today on the assumption that work means employment. With the shift from employment to ownwork, that assumption will have to be abandoned. In Chapter 7 we saw that this implies important changes in the concepts of macro-economics. New indicators of economic performance and social wellbeing will have to be developed, no longer based on the assumption that all paid work has value and all unpaid work does not. This needs to be put in hand urgently,

as an important feature of 'the new economics'. At the same time, we have to bear in mind that the age of economics has coincided with the age of employment and more generally with the industrial age. We should be aware of the possibility that economics may not survive the transition to the post-employment, post-industrial age, at least in its present form.

Throughout the social sciences it will be necessary to question whether work should continue to be taken as meaning employment. As in other fields, a systematic review of the implications of this is called for. However, in parallel with other fields, academic inertia and academic vested interests in the status quo make such a systematic review unlikely until the shift from employment to ownwork has become more commonplace. So meanwhile, in parallel with other items on the ownwork agenda, it will be a top priority for pioneers of alternative thinking to open up the field.[14]

A specific example of a subject where this applies is 'quality of working life' (QWL).[15] The academics and consultants who have been active in this field have hitherto limited their interest to the QWL for people in employment – so that, for example, QWL is now closely associated with the field of research and consultancy known as 'organisation development' or OD. It is probably too cynical to say that this is because employers are the only people willing to pay academics and consultants to look at QWL. The underlying reason is because it has been generally assumed that employment is the only kind of working life that matters. But now, as the shift to ownwork proceeds, interest in QWL will have to shift away from situations in which employees work, to those in which work is organised in other, more self-directed ways.

Key Institutions
The response of the institutions most closely affected by the ownwork agenda will help to determine whether the worldwide crisis of unemployment is successfully surmounted, and whether the transition to a post-employment age is accomplished in reasonably good order. Those institutions are: employing organisations; government departments and agencies; financial institutions; trade unions; and the professions, such as architecture, planning, and education, which directly

influence the context for work and people's capabilities for doing it. The practical question is not so much about the extent to which these institutions may be expected to take positive initiatives to accelerate the shift to ownwork. More importantly, it is about the extent to which they will prove willing and able to remove the huge variety of obstacles with which they now hinder the spread of ownwork, for example by giving tax depreciation allowances and investment grants to employing organisations but not to self-organised workers, by administering personal taxes and benefits in such a way that the poverty trap is created, by designing the built environment to suit an employment-based society, by imposing criteria of educational success which discourage practical self-reliance, or by insisting that certain kinds of work have to be done by certified or unionised employees.

In general, *employing organisations* will probably continue to encourage the trend towards ownwork, as they have done in the last few years. They will continue to reduce the numbers of their full-time employees, partly by using machines instead of labour, partly by employing more part-time workers, and partly by contracting work out instead of doing it in-house. Managerial inertia and gut resistance to change will no doubt slow things down a bit. For a time, top managers and other key workers will probably continue to be employed full-time, and to regard themselves as the core, and other workers as the periphery, of the business they are in. This may apply a kind of cultural brake to progress for a while. But this will probably soon be offset by the spread of the new cultural values, centred around the principle of personal autonomy, which ownwork will represent. All in all, I expect large employers and the representative organisations of employers to play an increasingly positive part in removing existing obstacles to the wider spread of ownwork. The challenge to business management will be one which many managers will welcome, as they begin to explore more systematically than hitherto the scope for a larger role for ownwork in their own businesses, the obstacles to moving in that direction, and how those obstacles might be removed.

Departments and agencies of central and local government are likely, in general, to be less flexible in their response. In their case, managerial inertia and gut resistance to change will tend to be reinforced by the political context in which they operate. In principle, the shift from employment to ownwork will imply a general shift of emphasis towards measures that enable people and localities to meet more of their needs for themselves. As we saw in Chapter 10, the prospect of such a shift is experienced as a threat by most of today's power structures, including all mainstream political parties.[16] This means that, even if government managers want to introduce enabling policies in place of dependency-creating policies or policies of neglect, they will often find difficulty in getting political support for them. Nonetheless, I expect increasing numbers of government officials to become sympathetic to the ownwork agenda, and supportive of it, in the next few years. This will be partly because they are pushed in that direction by the pressure of events, partly because they themselves see that the future lies that way, and partly because the ownwork agenda and the development and implementation of enabling policies will – paradoxically – open up a wide range of new opportunities for career achievement in every branch of the public service. The policy implications of the shift from employment to ownwork will offer a new lease of life to policy researchers, and to institutes like (in Britain) the Royal Institute of Public Administration and the Policy Studies Institute.

In general, *financial institutions* may be less sympathetic to the ownwork agenda than employers or public servants. There is an underlying conflict between the idea of a society based on the money-making ethos of financial institutions and the idea of a society based on the principles of ownwork. This is bound to reinforce the normal inertia and gut resistance to change among the majority of people managing financial businesses. Moreover, people who gravitate into the management of financial institutions tend to be less responsive to social issues and to impending social change than people who manage other, less abstract types of manufacturing and service industries.

Fortunately, however, there are many exceptions to this generalisation. And – paradoxically again – the shift to ownwork will, as we saw in Chapter 9, offer a widening range of new opportunities for profitable investment to the alert financial managers who have a nose for what is happening.

There is bound to be a growing demand for financial business analysts to identify growth points for new financial opportunities of this kind. Systematic analyses of the whole range of ownwork projects, personal and local, may be needed, to identify what new ways of providing finance for these projects will have to be developed.

Of all the institutions affected by the shift to ownwork, the *trade unions* may find it most difficult to respond in positive ways. As we saw in Chapter 8, they are locked firmly into a defensive pattern of response. However, there are trade union leaders who are beginning to realise that this must change. For example, Clive Jenkins and Barrie Sherman argue that unemployed people should be helped to make good use of their leisure. They see trade unions representing the unemployed, and spending more time than at present on non-wage bargaining. They think the trade unions should also be prepared to bargain on behalf of the sick and the disabled, the new co-operatives, and single-parent families, all at both national and local levels. Their suggestion that unions should represent the interest of those in receipt of the 'social wage' raises the possibility of the trade union movement eventually negotiating on behalf of all citizens about the level of the Guaranteed Basic Income (GBI). But leaving that aside, recognition by the trade union movement that it has responsibilities to people outside employment, as well as in it, seems bound to grow. Pressing the claims of such people to adequate financial provision from the state will be one way of exercising these responsibilities, but by itself it will not be enough.

It will be necessary for the trade union movement to accept the inevitable contraction of formal employment, and to strive to ensure it takes place on terms that are favourable to affected employees. This will involve the negotiation of terms for flexible work patterns, including part-time work, early retirement, sabbaticals, etc., as well as terms for redundancy. It will also involve more active representation of the interests of part-time workers than has been customary, and more active support for people who are looking for part-time jobs.

Moreover, in a further extension of their present role, trade unions might be able to represent the interests of people working outside formal employment, and give assistance to people trying to organise their ownwork. Trade unions might provide technical and legal support and advice for such people. Perhaps they might regulate the qualifications of independent workers (as the old guilds used to do), and so provide potential customers with an assurance of the standard of work on offer. Trade unions could press for changes in government policy and regulations (for example on taxation and social security and on planning) that discourage or hinder people working on their own account. They could press for land and resources to be made more readily available for people who want to do such things as grow their own food, build their own homes, or start their own co-operative and community enterprises.

Somewhere in the trade union movement today there may be young, energetic men and women who are aware of these possibilities and who are thinking them out. If so, they will lead the trade union movement into the 21st century. If not, the role of trade unions seems certain to dwindle, as the shift from employment to ownwork gathers pace. The passing away of employment as the dominant mode of work will then be like a tide going out. It will leave the trade union movement stranded on the shore of history.

As we have seen in Chapters 4 and 11, the ownwork agenda will pose a challenge to many of the *professions*, such as architecture, planning and teaching whose practices have become firmly rooted in the needs of an employment-based society. The pattern of response will tend to repeat itself from one of these professions to another: first, automatic resistance to change among most of the older and more established members, accompanied by an upsurge of interest among younger, more thoughtful, more energetic members; second, practical demonstrations that professional knowhow can be effectively applied to the new needs, and that the shift to ownwork is actually opening up new opportunities for the profession; third, acceptance by the profession that ownwork is a fact of life and that they can handle it; fourth, claims by the profession that enabling people to work for themselves has, in fact, always been one of their main aims. We are at present somewhere near the beginning of the second of these stages. In other words, an exciting new future is just opening up for architects, planners and teachers who can grasp what ownwork involves and can create their own new agenda around it.

Conclusion

What work has been done, and how work has been organised, have differed from one historical period to another. But work, whatever its form, and however organised, has always been a central activity in most people's lives.

For the future two things seem certain. First, we are moving out of one historical period into another. This will bring great changes in what people do as work and in how work is organised. The age in which employment has been the dominant form of work is coming to an end. Second, many people – probably most – will continue to want to work. They will want their lives to be centred around activity that is valuable and useful, and meets needs – their own and other people's. So, although there will no doubt continue to be many jobs, and although many people will no doubt enjoy more leisure than in the past, the real challenge is to move – as understandingly and with as little disruption and distress as we can – to new kinds of work and new ways of organising work.

The key is to understand this as a move to ownwork – to forms of work, paid and unpaid, which people organise and control for themselves; in order to achieve purposes which they perceive as their own; as individuals, in groups, and in the localities in which they live. This transition from employment to ownwork can be seen as the next stage in the progression towards freedom, responsibility, and fuller participation in the life of society, that was marked at earlier historical times by the transitions from slavery to serfdom, and then from serfdom to employment. It can also be seen, by those who look at things this way, as one aspect of the next step towards fuller personal participation by human beings in the universal process of evolution.

But, as I said at the outset, effective responses to the unemployment crisis must be practical, as well as visionary. In Part 4 I have touched on some of the practicalities of the transition to ownwork. I hope that readers will have found it helpful to have had these practicalities placed in the historical and political context outlined in Parts 2 and 3. I hope also that the Ownwork Checklist at Appendix 2 will help readers, whether they agree with the idea of ownwork or not, to think about the practical implications of a move towards it, either for themselves personally or for society as a whole.

However, let me make it plain that neither I nor anyone else at this point can see in detail how the ownwork agenda will be carried out. We cannot now describe precisely what new arrangements should be brought in across the board – as aspects of the transition to ownwork – for enabling people to receive incomes, to have acccess to land, and so on. The fact is that the transition will not be achieved by vast numbers of us carrying out en masse a single comprehensive plan laid down in advance as if by a single super-employer; rather, it will be achieved by means appropriate to the end. In other words, it will be achieved by more and more people deciding to do their own thing, finding ways to do it, and thereby helping to move things in the right direction.

There is a well-known saying 'Think globally, act locally'. In the present context this means that we should try to understand the crisis of work globally. We should see it as a symptom of the decline of a historical era in which the employment way of organising work has been one of the forms of dependency created by a dependency-creating society. We should thus understand it as a historic opportunity for a liberation of work. Then, informed by this understanding, we should find practical ways to act that are consistent with it, and that we ourselves are capable of initiating and carrying through.

The new work order will not be brought in by mass action, responding to the requirements of a bureaucratic programme and reflecting the factory mentality of the employment age. It will come in as growing numbers of people, conscious of sharing the same vision of the future of work and of travelling the same journey towards it, find new ways of organising work for themselves and enabling one another to do the same.

A Note on Paradigm Shifts

A paradigm shift is the change that takes place from time to time in a basic belief or assumption (or in a constellation of basic beliefs or assumptions) underlying our perceptions and actions. It can be seen as the cultural equivalent of an evolutionary leap. A well-known example is the shift, which took place in the 16th and 17th centuries and is associated with the names of Copernicus and Galileo, from the view that the sun goes round the earth to the view that the earth goes round the sun.

The concept of a paradigm shift arose from studies of the history of science. It was given currency by T.S. Kuhn in his book, *The Structure of Scientific Revolutions*.[1] Kuhn examined

> the major turning points in scientific development associated with the names of Copernicus, Newton, Lavoisier, and Einstein. More clearly than most other episodes in the history of at least the physical sciences, these display what all scientific revolutions are about. Each of them necessitated the community's rejection of one time-honoured scientific theory in favour of another incompatible with it. Each produced a consequent shift in the problems available for scientific scrutiny and in the standards by which the profession determined what should count as an admissible problem or as a legitimate problem-solution. And each transformed the scientific imagination in ways that we shall ultimately need to describe as a transformation of the world within which scientific work was done. Such changes, together with the controversies that almost always accompany them, are the defining characteristics of scientific revolutions.

Kuhn concluded that

> the successive transition from one paradigm to another via revolution is the actual developmental pattern of mature

science . . . When an individual or group first produces a syn-
thesis able to attract most of the next generation's practitioners, the older schools gradually disappear. In part, their
disappearance is caused by their members' conversion to the
new paradigm. But there are always some men who cling to
one or another of the old views, and they are simply read out of
the profession which thereafter ignores. their work.

The prevailing paradigm provides the agenda for all the on-
going activities of routine practitioners of science. As the
paradigm shift occurs, those activities change their direction
in accordance with the new paradigm.

In very much the same way as Kuhn described for science,
prevailing paradigms provide the context for routine activity
in non-scientific affairs, and shifts take place from one
paradigm to another. For example, human beings can see
themselves as outside nature, whence they can observe it,
dominate it and exploit it; or, by contrast, they can feel themselves to be an integral part of nature. One aspect of the
change of direction to the SHE future will be a shift from the
first of these two paradigms to the second, i.e. from a scientific
and economic view of nature to an ecological and spiritual
view. Again, the dominant paradigm in economic affairs may
be one of maximising and expansion; or it may be one of suf-
ficiency and balance. A shift from the first to the second of
these two paradigms will also be part of the transition to the
SHE future.

An Ownwork Checklist
Twenty Questions for Discussion
and Further Exploration

Personal
1. How might I find ways of:
    – working
    – managing my money, time, space, resources
    – acquiring skills and experience
    – changing my lifestyle
that would enable me to call my life my own and participate actively in my local economy?

2. What kinds of help, advice and support would I need for this, and where should I look for them?

Local
3. As people belonging to a particular locality, how could we find ways of:
    – working
    – managing our money and resources
that would enable us to meet a greater proportion of our own local needs by using our own local work and our own local money and resources?

4. What kinds of help, advice and support would we need for this, and where should we look for them?

Financial
5. How could a Guaranteed Basic Income (GBI) be financed?

6. What interim changes in personal benefits and taxation, short of a GBI could be introduced, in order to relax the poverty trap and enable recipients of benefits to do useful work for themselves?

7.   (a) Should a land tax be introduced, in order to:
      – bring down the price of land
      – make land more easily available for people who need it
        for work
      – bring unused land into productive use?
      (b) If so, what form should it take?

8.   Government grants and tax allowances now paid to
employers discriminate in favour of corporate production
and against production in the informal economy, in favour of
employment and against ownwork. How could this discrimination be removed?

9.   What changes could be made in the existing financial
system, in order to:
      – distribute newly created money and credit to all
        citizens as part of their basic income
      – provide new channels for investment in local projects
        and the local economy
      – provide new ways of financing the purchase of land
      – encourage people to become less, rather than more,
        dependent on money and credit
      – safeguard against the worst consequences of a possible
        financial collapse in the next ten years?

New Legal and Financial Structures
10.   What new forms of co-operative and community-based
enterprises and trusts could be developed as vehicles for:
      – local socio-economic activities
      – land purchase and land tenure for such activities?

Employers
11.   What range of strategies are available to employers:
      – to become less dependent on employees for getting
        work done
      – to reorientate existing employees towards ownwork?

Technologies
12.   What action can businesses take to establish themselves
in the growing market for small technologies that cater for personal and local ownwork?

13. What action could government agencies take to ensure that the required small technologies are researched and developed in good time?

Physical Design and Planning
14. How could architects and planners be encouraged to design and plan physical space and the built environment, to cater for ownwork rather than for patterns of living based on employment?

Education, Training and Leisure
15. What changes could be made by the professions and authorities responsible for education and training and for providing facilities for leisure, to recognise the growing importance of ownwork in people's lives?

Central Government
16. What changes would be needed in central government policies of all kinds to facilitate the shift to ownwork and reduce people's dependence on employment?

Local Government
17. As Question 16, but for local government.

Trade Unions
18. Could trade unions contribute positively to the shift from employment to ownwork? If so, in what particular ways?

Research and Consultancy
19. What new openings for research and consultancy arise out of the previous questions, and also out of the new thinking in the economic and social sciences required by the concept of work as ownwork rather than as employment?

Public and Political Discussion
20. What could I do to raise public and political awareness of the key importance of ownwork as a response to the unemployment crisis, and as the basis for a better future for work?

Notes and References

Introduction

(1)   Reported in the United Nations publication *Development Forum*, November 1982.

(2)   The concept of 'another development' was articulated in the 1975 Dag Hammarskjold Report 'What Now? Another Development'; in *Another Development: Approaches and Strategies*, ed. Marc Nerfin, 1977; and in subsequent issues of *Development Dialogue*; all published by the Dag Hammarskjold Foundation, Uppsala, Sweden. Regular issues of the *IFDA Dossier* from the International Foundation for Development Alternatives, Nyon, Switzerland, have encouraged wide international participation in the discussion.

(3)   In particular, the outcome of two Turning Point meetings in 1980 was published as Turning Point Paper No. 1 on 'The Redistribution of Work'. Major contributions were made by Charles Handy (then Warden of St. George's House, Windsor Castle) and Sheila Rothwell (Director of Employment Studies, Henley). I recommend Charles Handy's subsequent book, *The Future of Work*, Basil Blackwell, 1984. (Turning Point is an international network of people who share a common understanding that humankind is at a historical turning point. Address: The Old Bakehouse, Cholsey, Near Wallingford, Oxfordshire OX10 9NU).

The Woodbrooke College conference on the future of work in September 1982 led to the publication of *Turn A New Leaf: Six Essays On Work*, Friends House, London, 1983. Among the contributors was Guy Dauncey, whose two books, *The Unemployment Handbook*, 1981, and *Nice Work If You Can Get It*, 1983 – both published by the National Extension College – I also recommend.

(4) James Robertson, *The Sane Alternative: A Choice of Futures*, rev. ed. Robertson, 1983. As I said there, Gurth Higgin's 'Scarcity, Abundance and Depletion: The Challenge to Continuing Management Education', Inaugural Lecture, Loughborough University of Technology, 1975, provided an important stimulus to my thinking about the future of work.

Chapter 1
(1) Detailed references are given in *The Sane Alternative*, see Introduction, Note (4).
(2) Amory Lovins, *Soft Energy Paths*, Penguin, 1977.
(3) For example, David Bleakley, *Work: The Shadow and the Substance*, SCM Press, 1983, argues for alternative approaches to employment and unemployment which will transcend the conventional work ethic.

Chapter 2
(1) This four-sector model emerged from an international discussion at Windsor Castle in 1979 on the future of business management. See my report on 'The Changing Expectations Of Society' in *Management for the 21st Century*, Kluwer Nijhoff, 1982.
(2) Tom Stonier, *The Wealth of Information: A Profile of the Post-Industrial Economy*, Thames Methuen, 1983. Stonier says that in 25 years 'it will take no more than 10% of the labour force to provide us with all our material needs'.
(3) 'There was virtual unanimity that full employment has gone for good.' From the report on 'The Future of Work' by OPUS (10 Golders Rise, London NW4), after the Work and Society 'Talkabout' in West Yorkshire in October/November 1983.
(4) For a readable account of Kondratieff cycles see Robert Beckman, *Downwave: Surviving the Second Great Depression*, Pan, 1983. Also see Christopher Freeman's 'Science, Technology and Unemployment', Paper No. 1 in Science, Technology and Public Policy, from Science Policy Research Unit, Sussex University, 1982.
(5) See the references to slavery in Adam Smith's *Wealth of Nations* and Karl Marx's *Capital*.

Chapter 3

(1) Useful background on the work of the household and community in pre-industrial society will be found in Edward Shorter's *The Making Of The Modern Family*, Fontana, 1977; and Peter Laslett's *The World We Have Lost*, Methuen, 1971.

(2) Ivan Illich, *Tools for Conviviality*, Calder and Boyars, 1973.

(3) 'The self-made man was the ideal entrepreneur, the man without any initial property or patronage, no education other than self-education, or any advantage other than native talent, who by self-help and force of character made his way to wealth and status.' Harold Perkin, *The Origins of Modern English Society, 1780–1880*, RKP, 1969.

(4) 'From one end of Europe to the other, young unmarried women in the 19th century were rejecting traditional occupations in favour of paid employment . . . Young women in particular who left home to accept work in London were not so much responding to economic opportunity as to a means of independence from the often severe restraints on behaviour inherent in rural family life, dominated by the Victorian paterfamilias.' E. Shorter, *Making of the M.F.*

(5) Disraeli, *Sybil; Or The Two Nations*, OUP World Classic, 1981 (first pub. 1845). Also see Karl Polanyi's *The Great Transformation*, Beacon, 1957.

(6) Christopher Hill, *Reformation To Industrial Revolution*, Penguin, 1969.

(7) All quotations in this paragraph are from C. Hill, *Reformation*.

(8) E.P. Thompson, *The Making Of The English Working Class*, Penguin, 1968.

(9) Examples of brutality will be found in E.P. Thompson, *Making of the E.W.C.*

(10) Graham Marshall, *The Best Years Of Their Lives: Schooling, Work And Unemployment In Oldfield*, William Temple Foundation, Manchester Business School, 1980.

(11) Studs Terkel, *Working*, Penguin, 1977.

(12) 'Work in America', Special Task Force Report to the Secretary of Health, Education and Welfare,

Cambridge, Mass., 1973, quoted by Harry Braverman, *Labor And Monopoly Capital: The Degradation Of Work In The 20th Century*, Monthly Review Press, 1974.

Chapter 4

(1)   Daniel Deudney and Christopher Flavin, *Renewable Energy: The Power To Choose*, Norton/Worldwatch, 1983.

(2)   Humanistic psychology and other 'new age' thinking about personal growth emphasises the importance of unblocking people's psychic energies and releasing them into creative channels. See, for example, the index references to 'energies' in Roberto Assagioli's *Psychosynthesis*, Turnstone, 1975.

(3)   Further reading on technology 'as if people matter' is in E.F. Schumacher's *Good Work*, Cape, 1979; and George McRobie's *Small Is Possible*, Cape, 1981.

(4)   Marion Shoard, *The Theft of the Countryside*, Temple Smith, 1980.

(5)   *The Global 2000 Report to the President: Entering the 21st Century*, Penguin, 1982, concluded that 'if present trends continue, the world in 2000 will be more crowded, more polluted, less stable ecologically, and more vulnerable to disruption than the world we live in now', and that 'prompt and vigorous changes in public policy are needed to avoid or minimise these problems before they become unmanageable'.

(6)   The Town and Country Planning Association (17 Carlton House Terrace, London SW1Y 5AS) and its journal, *Town and Country Planning*, are a valuable source of information and ideas. So are John Turner, author of *Housing by People*, Marion Boyars, 1976, and his colleagues at AHAS (PO Box 397, London E8 1BA). Also see John Adams' *Transport Planning: Vision and Practice*, RKP, 1981.

(7)   Leisure studies, including academic research and business consultancy, have mushroomed in recent years. See, for example, Stanley Parker's *Leisure and Work*, Allen and Unwin, 1983. I have learned much from W.H. Martin and S. Mason, whose *Leisure and Work: The Choices for 1991 and 2001*, Leisure Consultants, 1982, provides a

good overview for readers from businesses and other organisations.

Chapter 5

(1) Max Weber, *The Protestant Ethic and the Spirit of Capitalism*, Unwin, 1930.

(2) R.H. Tawney, *Religion and the Rise of Capitalism*, Penguin, 1938.

(3) Quoted in M. Weber, *Protestant Ethic*.

(4) E.P. Thompson, *Making of the E.W.C.*

(5) Quotations in this paragraph and the next are from M. Weber, *Protestant Ethic*.

(6) A good short account of Cartesian dualism is in Fritjof Capra's *The Turning Point*, Wildwood House, 1982. References to Cartesian dualism in the context of economics will be found in Hazel Henderson's *The Politics of the Solar Age: Alternatives to Economics*, Anchor Doubleday, 1981; and Guy Dauncey's *Nice Work If You Can Get It*, National Extension College, 1983. In brief, Descartes founded modern science and philosophy on the assumption that reality consisted of two separate realms – mind (*res cogitans*) and matter (*res extensa*). His method involved the application of mathematical reasoning to indubitable observations. Later scientists came to assume that scientific knowledge must be based on the use of this method in the study of matter, and expelled other insights, including moral, spiritual and intuitive understanding, from the realm of knowledge. Following this pattern, economists have studied only the formal economy, and have relegated the informal economy to the realm of superstition, hearsay and old wives' tales.

(7) Quotations in this paragraph and the next are from R.H. Tawney, *Religion*.

(8) Quotations in this paragraph and the next are from M. Weber, *Protestant Ethic*.

(9) 'Laborem Exercens', Encyclical Letter of The Supreme Pontiff John Paul II on Human Work, Catholic Truth Society, 1981.

(10) Karl Marx, *Capital*, Vol. 1, Penguin, 1976.

(11) Kahlil Gibran, *The Prophet*, Heinemann, 1926. The

prophet is here responding to a ploughman's request, 'Speak to us of Work.'

(12) William Morris, 'Useful Work Versus Useless Toil', 1885, reprinted in *William Morris: Selected Writings and Designs*, ed. Asa Briggs, Penguin, 1962.

(13) E. F. Schumacher, *Good Work*.

(14) Bertrand Russell, 'In Praise of Idleness', 1932, reprinted in *Why Work? Arguments for the Leisure Society*, ed. Vernon Richards, Freedom Press, 1983.

(15) A Haitian proverb quoted by Clive Jenkins and Barrie Sherman in *The Collapse of Work*, Eyre Methuen, 1979, and in *The Leisure Shock*, Eyre Methuen, 1981.

(16) Marx described his vision of communism as follows: 'In place of the old bourgeois society, with its classes and class antagonisms, we shall have an association in which the free development of each is the condition for the free development of all.' Communist Manifesto, 1848.

Chapter 6

(1) Jacques Monod, *Chance and Necessity*, Collins, 1972.

(2) J.E. Lovelock, *Gaia: A new look at life on Earth*, OUP, 1979.

(3) Chief Seattle's oration is quoted in Duane Elgin's *Voluntary Simplicity*, Morrow, 1981.

(4) Fritjof Capra, *The Tao of Physics*, Wildwood House, 1975.

(5) For example, Manfred Max-Neef, *From The Outside Looking In: Experiences in Barefoot Economics,* Dag Hammarskjold Foundation, Uppsala, 1982.

(6) For a balanced discussion of the possibilities, see the chapter on participatory democracy in C.B. Macpherson's *The Life and Times of Liberal Democracy*, OUP, 1977. Also see the chapter on 'Politics' in Kirkpatrick Sale's *Human Scale*, Secker and Warburg, 1980.

(7) For an overview, see Marilyn Ferguson's *The Aquarian Conspiracy*, Tarcher, 1980. Also see Brian Inglis's *Natural Medicine*, Collins, 1979.

(8) The word 'cosmogenesis' is used by Pierre Teilhard de Chardin in *The Phenomenon of Man*, Collins, 1959, and other works, to describe the process by which the universe evolves out of matter into life and conscious-

ness and on towards superconsciousness and divinity.

(9) A good account of this is in Peter Russell's *The Awakening Earth: Our Next Evolutionary Leap*, RKP, 1982.

(10) A good discussion of 'the conviction that the human species should and will conquer nature through the progress of modern science and technology' is in William Leiss's *The Limits To Satisfaction*, Marion Boyars, 1978. A well-known advocate of human mastery over nature for the 'relief of the inconvenience of man's estate' was Francis Bacon in the early 17th century.

(11) These findings on 'The New Consumer Values' were communicated by Paul E. Shay to the Annual Conference of the British Advertising Association in April 1978. A fuller account is in Arnold Mitchell's *Who We Are: The Values and Lifestyles of Americans*, Macmillan, 1983.

(12) D. Elgin, *Voluntary Simplicity*.

(13) Daniel Yankelovich, *New Rules: Searching for Self-Fulfilment in a World Turned Upside Down*, 1982; and *Work and Human Values: An International Report on Jobs in the 1980s and 1990s*, Aspen Institute for Humanistic Studies, Stockholm, 1983.

(14) Erich Fromm, *The Sane Society*, RKP, 1963.

(15) Lionel Tiger and Robin Fox, *The Imperial Animal*, Paladin, 1974.

(16) Virginia Woolf, *A Room Of One's Own*, Penguin, 1945.

(17) Marshall Sahlins, *Stone Age Economics*, Tavistock, 1974. Sahlins is quoting from a study by Richard Lee.

(18) See E. Shorter, *Making of the M.F.*

(19) For the relative degradation of women's work brought about by industrialisation see Ivan Illich's *Shadow Work* and *Gender*, Marion Boyars, 1981 and 1983. The same process is accelerating in third world countries today. See, for example, Valentina Borremans' *Technique and Women's Toil*, Tecnopolitica (Apdo. 479, Cuernavaca, Mexico), 1982.

(20) *Women, Work and Family in the Soviet Union*, ed. Gail W. Lapidus, Sharpe, 1982.

(21) Kathleen Newland, *The Sisterhood of Man*, Norton, 1979.

(22) André Gorz, *Farewell to the Working Class; An Essay on Post-*

Industrial Socialism, Pluto Press, 1982.

(23)　Virginia Novarra, *Women's Work, Men's Work*, Marion Boyars, 1980. See also the chapters on work in Sheila Rowbotham's *Woman's Consciousness: Man's World*, Penguin, 1973.

(24)　I owe this point to Sheila Rothwell, 'Flexible Working Patterns for the Future'. Information about this and other papers given at The Other Economic Summits in June 1984 and April 1985 is available from TOES, 42 Warriner Gardens, London SW11 4DU.

Chapter 7

(1)　The quotations in this paragraph and the next two are from R.H. Tawney, *Religion*.

(2)　John Locke, *Second Treatise of Government*.

(3)　Adam Smith, *The Wealth of Nations*, Penguin, 1970.

(4)　K. Marx, *Capital*, Vol. 1.

(5)　John Stuart Mill, *Principles of Political Economy*, Longmans Green, 1926. (I owe this reference, and reference (7) below, to William J. Barber's useful *A History of Economic Thought*, Penguin, 1967.)

(6)　'Laborem Exercens', see Chapter 5, Note (9).

(7)　This and the following quotation are from Alfred Marshall, *Principles of Economics*, Vol. 1, Macmillan, 1961.

(8)　Aubrey Jones, *The New Inflation: The Politics of Prices and Incomes*, Andre Deutsch, 1973.

Chapter 8

(1)　E.P. Thompson, *Making of the E.W.C.*

(2)　H. Braverman, *Labor and Monopoly Capital*.

(3)　Mike Cooley, *Architect or Bee, The Human Technology Relationship*, Langley Technical Services, 1980.

(4)　I. Illich, *Shadow Work*.

(5)　Hilary Wainwright and Dave Elliott, *The Lucas Plan: A New Trade Unionism in the Making?*, Allison and Busby, 1982.

(6)　M. Cooley, *Architect or Bee*.

(7)　Robert Jungk, *The Everyman Project: Resources for a Humane Future*, Thames and Hudson, 1976.

(8)　A. Gorz, *Farewell to the Working Class*.

(9)   Leszek Kolakowski, *Main Currents of Marxism*, Vol. 2, OUP, 1978.
(10)   Jeremy Seabrook, *Unemployment*, Paladin, 1982.

Chapter 9
(1)   Existing examples include: Mercury Provident Society, Orlingbury House, Lewes Road, Forest Row, Sussex RH18 5AA; Calvert Social Investment Fund, 1700 Pennsylvania Avenue NW, Washington DC 20006, USA.
(2)   David Cadman: 'Towards An Ecology Of Finance', *Town and Country Planning*, September, 1983. Bob Swann's (Box 76, RD3 Great Barrington, MA 01230, USA) 'Bookshelf' includes useful material on 'community banking'. URBED (Urban Economic Development, 99 Southwark Street, London SE1 0JF) and the Foundation for Alternatives (The Rookery, Adderbury, Banbury, Oxfordshire) are both concerned with new ways of financing local initiatives.
(3)   David Cadman and James Robertson, 'Before the dinosaur became extinct . . .', *The Guardian*, 2 December 1982.
(4)   No lasting solution to the international financial crisis, highlighted in the past few years by the debt problems of countries such as Poland, Mexico and Brazil, is in sight. Current agricultural land values are artificially high owing to agricultural support policies (such as the Common Agricultural Policy in the EEC) which are financially and politically unsustainable, and also owing to farming practices which are likely to be scientifically and economically unsustainable in the long run – see, for example, Richard Body's *Agriculture: The Triumph and the Shame* and *Farming in the Clouds*, both published by Temple Smith, 1982 and 1984.
(5)   James Robertson, *Profit Or People? The New Social Role of Money*, Calder and Boyars, 1974.

Chapter 10
(1)   This new class exists in communist as well as capitalist countries, as the Yugoslav writer Milovan Djilas was one of the first to point out in his books, *The New Class* and

The Unperfect Society: Beyond The New Class, Unwin, 1972.
(2)   Notable examples of this trend are the activities of Ralph Nader in the United States, and in the United Kingdom of Des Wilson, who has in recent years led successful pressure groups on housing, the environment and open government.
(3)   Already the question of how far to operate through the existing political processes and how far to withdraw from them has arisen among supporters of the Green Party in Germany and the Ecology Party in Britain. See Jonathon Porritt: *Seeing Green: The Politics of Ecology Explained*, Blackwell, 1984; and Fritjof Capra and Charlene Spretnak, *Green Politics: The Global Promise* (British ed.), Hutchinson, 1984.
(4)   See, for example, the account of the Reform Bill crisis of 1832 in E.P. Thompson, *Making of the E.W.C.* For a good account of the process of social, economic and political change in 19th-century Britain see H. Perkin, *Origins of M.E.S.*

Chapter 11
(1)   A useful source of information is: BURN (British Unemployment Resources Network, c/o Birmingham Settlement, 318 Summer Lane, Birmingham B19 6RL). Also Guy Dauncey's two books – see Introduction, Note (3). Professor Denis Pym of the London Business School has suggested, e.g. in a recent paper on 'The Case for the Bricoleur', that a new ethic of resourcefulness reflects a growing awareness that, in matters of personal responsibility, dignity and control over our own affairs, the status of self-employment is now preferable to employment.
(2)   The Briarpatch Network in San Francisco is an interesting example of co-operation and mutual support between small local enterprises established by lifestyle and social entrepreneurs.
(3)   Alan Bollard, *An Alternative Industrial Framework for the UK*, Intermediate Technology Publications (9 King Street, London WC2), 1983.
(4)   However, there are signs that leading business managers

may be moving in this direction. See, for example, Francis Kinsman's report in 'The New Agenda', Spencer Stuart Management Consultants, London, 1983, of conversations with 30 leading business people.

(5)   Philip Toogood, *The Head's Tale*, Dialogue Publications, 1984; and A.G. Watts, *Education, Unemployment and the Future of Work*, Open University, 1983.

(6)   In Britain this has been initiated by Alec Dickson and Nicholas Stacey of Youth Call (c/o Social Services Department, Springfield, Maidstone, Kent).

(7)   See Chapter 4, Note (6).

(8)   For a fuller account of the developments mentioned in this chapter see Charles Handy *The Future of Work*. Relevant information is also published in the Work and Society newsletter (56 Britton Street, London EC1M 5NA); in the newsletter of the European Centre for Work and Society (PO Box 3073, 6202 NB Maastricht, Holland); and in various publications from Jobs and Society (Aspen Institute for Humanistic Studies, Stockholm).

Chapter 12

(1)   These were the assumptions underlying the Beveridge Report of 1942, on which the post-war welfare state in Britain has been based.

(2)   Useful references are: Minutes of Evidence (pp. 420 and 424) to the House of Commons Treasury and Civil Service Committee, Session 1982–83, Third Special Report, 'The Structure of Personal Income Taxation and Income Support', pub. December 1982 by HMSO; Keith Roberts's *Automation, Unemployment and the Distribution of Income*, European Centre for Work and Society – see Chapter 11, Note (8) – 1982; Anne Miller's 'The Economic Implications of Basic Income Schemes', paper for The Other Economic Summit, 1984 – see Chapter 6, (Note (24); Robert Theobald's *An Alternative Future for America*, Chicago, 1968; and Professor Willem Albeda's 'Reflections on the future of full employment', *Labour and Society*, Vol. 8, No. 1, 1983.

(3)   The guaranteed basic income scheme is not the same as, but has some features in common with, Social Credit.

An up-to-date introduction to Social Credit is Eric de Maré's 'A Matter of Life or Debt' (available from The Old House, Middle Duntisbourne, Near Cirencester, Glos GL7 7AR), 1983.

(4) A ten-year transition period is proposed by Keith Roberts – see Note (2) above.

(5) See Note (3) above.

(6) See Chapter 9, Note (4).

(7) Henry George, *Progress and Poverty*, Hogarth Press, 1966.

(8) Information on land trusts and community land banks is available from Bob Swann in North America and from the Foundation for Alternatives in Britain – see Chapter 9, Note (2). Also from Shann Turnbull (MAI Ltd., 33 Bligh Street, Sydney, Australia).

(9) In the United States The Rocky Mountain Institute (Drawer 248, Old Snowmass, Colorado 81654) is developing an Economic Renewal Project to provide a model for sustainable, locally-based, economic development on these lines.

(10) This was one of the proposals put forward at a conference on 'Technology Choice and the Future of Work', jointly organised by the British Association for the Advancement of Science and the Intermediate Technology Development Group on 22 November 1978 in London.

(11) See Chapter 9, Note (1) for two existing examples.

(12) Two examples are: The Centre for Alternative Technology at Machynlleth in Wales; and The Network for Alternative Technology and Technology Assessment (NATTA), based at the Open University.

(13) A wide variety of small initiatives already ranges from computer-skill centres to community farms for young unemployed people in cities, from small new community-organised schools and 'education otherwise' (home-based education) to appropriate technology courses in university engineering faculties, from farming courses on small-holdings to holidays devoted to study tours in rural development.

(14) Recent examples include: Hazel Henderson, *The Politics of the Solar Age: Alternatives to Economics*, Anchor Doubleday,

1981; and *Creating Alternative Futures: The End of Economics*, Berkley Windhover, 1978; Herman Daly, *Steady State Economics*, Freeman, 1977; Paul Hawken, *The Next Economy*, Holt, Rinehart and Winston, 1983; Mark Lutz and Kenneth Lux, *The Challenge of Humanistic Economics*, Benjamin Cummings, 1979; Scott Burns, *The Household Economy*, Beacon, 1975; Jonathan Gershuny, *After Industrial Society: The Emerging Self-Service Economy*, Macmillan, 1978; Joseph Huber (ed.), *Anders Arbeiten – Anders Wirtschaften*, Fischer Alternativ, Frankfurt, 1979; Graeme Shankland, *Our Secret Economy: The Response of the Informal Economy to the Rise of Mass Unemployment*, Anglo-German Foundation, London, 1980; William M. Nicholls and William A. Dyson, *The Informal Economy*, Vanier Institute of the Family, Ottawa, 1983; Ray Pahl, *Divisions of Labour*, Basil Blackwell, 1984; Hilda Scott: *Working Your Way to the Bottom: The Feminisation of Poverty*; Pandora, 1984; André Gorz: *Paths to Paradise: on the Liberation of Work*, Pluto, 1985; and Sean Cooney, *Work For All*, Inforecast, Dublin, 1985.

(15) A good short introduction to QWL will be found in Eric Trist's article 'Adapting to a Changing World' in the *Labour Gazette*, January 1978.

(16) This is well brought out by Anna Christensen, *Wage Labour as Social Order and Ideology*, Futures Studies Secretariat, Stockholm, 1984; and by Eric Miller, *Work and Creativity*, Tavistock Institute, London, Occasional Paper No. 6, 1983.

APPENDIX 1

(1) T.S. Kuhn, *The Structure of Scientific Revolutions*, University of Chicago Press, 1970.

Publications Index

After Industrial Society: The Emerging Self-Service Economy 208
Agriculture: The Triumph and the Shame 204
Alternative Future for America, An 206
Alternative Industrial Framework for the UK, An 205
Anders Arbeiten – Anders Wirtschaften 208
Another Development: Approaches and Strategies 196
Aquarian Conspiracy, The 201
Architect or Bee, the Human/Technology Relationship 203
Automation, Unemployment and the Distribution of Income 206
Awakening Earth, The: Our Next Evolutionary Leap 202

Best Years Of Their Lives, The 198

Capital, 197, 200, 203
Case for the Bricoleur 205
Challenge of Humanistic Economics, The 208
Chance and Necessity 201
Collapse of Work, The 123
Creating Alternative Futures: The End of Economics 207

Development Forum 196
Divisions of Labour 208
Downwave: Surviving the Second Great Depression 197

Economic Implications of Basic Income Schemes 206
Education, Unemployment and the Future of Work 206
Everyman Project, The: Resources for a Humane Future 203

Farewell to the Working Class: An Essay on Post-Industrial Socialism
    122, 202
Farming in the Clouds 204
Flexible Working Patterns for the Future 203
From the Outside Looking in: Experiences in Barefoot Economics 201
Future of Work, The 196, 206

Gaia: A New Look at Life on Earth 201
Gender 202
Global 2000 Report to the President: Entering the 21st Century 199
Good Work 199, 201
Great Transformation, The 198
Green Politics: The Global Promise 205

Head's Tale, The 206
History of Economic Thought, A 203
Household Economy, The 208
Housing by People 199
Human Scale 201

Imperial Animal, The 80, 202
In Praise of Idleness 201
Informal Economy, The 208

Labor and Monopoly Capital: The Degradation of Work in the 20th Century 199, 203
Laborem Exercens, 1981 encyclical 64, 200, 203
Leisure Shock, The 123
Leisure and Work 199
Leisure and Work: The Choices for 1991 and 2000 199
Life and Times of Liberal Democracy 201
Limits to Satisfaction 202
Lucas Plan, The: A New Trade Unionism in the Making 203

Main Currents of Marxism 204
Making of the English Working Class, The 109, 198, 200, 203
Making of the Modern Family, The 198
Management for the 21st Century 197
Matter of Life and Debt, A 206
Morris, William: Selected Writings and Designs 201

Natural Medicine 201
New Agenda, The 205
New Class, The 204
New Inflation, The: The Politics of Prices and Incomes 203
New Rules: Searching for Self-Fulfilment in a World Turned Upside Down 202
Next Economy, The 208
Nice Work if you can get it 196, 200

Origins of Modern English Society 198

Our Secret Economy: The Response of the Informal Economy to the Rise of Mass Unemployment 208

Paths to Paradise: on the Liberation of Work 208
Phenomenon of Man 201
Politics of the Solar Age: Alternatives to Economics 202, 207
Principles of Economics 203
Principles of Political Economy 203
Profit or People? The New Social Role of Money 204
Progress and Poverty 174, 206
Prophet, The 200
Protestant Ethic and the Spirit of Capitalism, The 200
Psychosynthesis 199

Redistribution of Work 196
Reflections on the future of Full Employment 206
Reformation to Industrial Revolution 198
Religion and the Rise of Capitalism 200, 203
Renewable Energy: The Power to Choose 199
Room of One's Own 81, 202

Sane Alternative, The: A Choice of Futures 197
Second Treatise of Government 203
Shadow Work 202, 203
Sisterhood of Man 202
Small Is Possible 199
Soft Energy Paths 197
Steady State Economics 207
Structure of Scientific Revolutions 191, 208
Sybil; Or The Two Nations 198

Tao of Physics, The 201
Technique and Women's Toil 202
Technology Choice and the Future of Work 207
The Sane Society 80
Theft of the Countryside, The 199
Tools for Conviviality 198
Transport Planning: Vision and Practice 199
Turn a New Leaf: Six Essays on Work 196
Turning Point, The 200

Unemployment 122, 204
Unemployment Handbook, The 196
Unperfect Society, The: Beyond the New Class 205

Useful Work Versus Useless Toil 201

Voluntary Simplicity 201

Wage Labour as Social Order and Ideology 208
Wealth of Nations, The 92, 197, 203
Wealth of Information, The 19, 197
What Now? Another Development 196
Who We Are: The Values and Lifestyles of Americans 202
Why Work? Arguments for the Leisure Society 201
Woman's Consciousness: Man's World 203
Women's Work, Men's Work 203
Women, Work and Family in the Soviet Union 84, 202
Work: The Shadow and the Substance 197
Work and Creativity 208
Work and Human Values 202
Work for All 208
Working 198
Working Your Way to the Bottom: The Feminisation of Poverty 208
World We Have Lost, The 198

Name Index

Adams, John 199
Albeda, Willem 206
Aquinas, St. Thomas 91
Assagioli, Roberto 199

Bacon, Francis 95
Barber, William J. 203
Baxter, Richard 58, 60, 61
Beckman, Robert 197
Beveridge Report 206
Bleakley, David 197
Body, Richard 204
Bollard, Alan 205
Borremans, Valentina 202
Braverman, Harry 112, 199, 203
Briarpatch Network 205
British Association for the Advancement of Science 207
British Steel Corporation 158
British Unemployment Resource Network (BURN) 152, 205
Burns, Scott 208
Business in the Community 159

Cadman, David 204
Calvert Social Investment Fund 204
Calvin, Calvinism 56–58
Camus, Albert 66
Capra, Fritjof 200, 201, 205
Catholic Church 56

Centre for Alternative Technology 207
Centre for Employment Initiatives 155
Centre for Urban and Regional Studies 179
Chartists 144
Christensen, Anna 208
Church Action With The Unemployed (CAWTU) 152
Co-operative Development Agencies 155
Common Agricultural Policy (CAP) 136, 174
Communist Manifesto (1848) 201
Community Programme 160, 162
Community Service Volunteers 163
Conservatives 138, 139, 142, 143
Cooley, Mike 112–113, 203
Cooney, Sean 208
Craigmillar Festival Society 153

Dag Hammarskjold Foundation 196
Daly, Herman 207
Dauncey, Guy 196, 200
Declaration of Independence 118
de Mare, Eric 206

Deudney, Daniel and Flavin, Christopher 199
Dickson, Alec 206
Disraeli 198
Djilas, Milovan 204
Douglas, C. H. 172

Easterhouse Festival Society 153
Ecology Party 143, 205
Elgin, Duane 77, 78, 201
Elliott, Dave 114, 203
Enterprise Allowance Scheme 162, 166
European Centre for Work and Society 206
European Economic Commission (EEC) 152, 161–162

Ferguson, Marilyn 201
Foundation for Alternatives 204, 207
Franklin, Benjamin 60
Freeman, Christopher 197
Fromm, Erich 80

Gaia 74, 75
George, Henry 174–176, 206
Gershuny, Jonathan 208
Gibran, Kahlil 65, 200
Gorz, Andre 86, 120, 122–124, 202, 203, 208
Green Party 205
Greentown Project 161, 164
Gulbenkian Foundation 153

Handy, Charles 196, 206
Hawken, Paul 208
Hegel 96
Henderson, Hazel 200, 207
Higgin, Gurth 197
Hill, Christopher 30, 198
Huber, Joseph 208

ICI 157, 158
Illich, Ivan 113, 198, 202, 203
Industrial Common Ownership Movement (ICOM) 155
Inglis, Brian 201
Institute of Local Government 179
Intermediate Technology Development Group (ITDG) 155
International Labour Office (I.L.O.) ix
International Foundation for Development Alternatives (IFDA), and IFDA Dossier 196
Ironbridge Gorge Museum Trust 154

Jenkins, Clive 123
Jobs and Society 206
Jones, Aubrey 102, 203
Jungk, Robert 115, 203

Kahn, Herman 4
Kelvin, Lord 100
Kinsman, Francis 205
Kolakowski, Leszek 121, 204
Kondratieff cycles 21, 22, 136, 138, 197
Kuhn, T. S. 191–192, 208

Labour 109, 120, 138, 139, 142, 143
Laslett, Peter 198
Leiss, William 202
Liberals 138, 142, 143
Lightmoor Project 161, 164
Locke, John 91, 92, 94, 203
Lovelock J. E. 201
Lovins, Amory 197
Lucas Aerospace 113–115
Luddites 111
Luther, 56–58

Lutz, Mark and Lux, Kenneth 208

Macpherson, C. B. 201
Manchester Business School 151
Manpower Services Commission 149, 151, 154, 160, 162, 163
Marshall, Alfred 99, 203
Marshall, Graham 198
Martin, W. H. and Mason, S. 199
Marx, Karl 23, 65, 91, 94–97, 121, 197, 200, 203
Max-Neef, Manfred 201
McRobie, George 199
Mercury Provident Society 204
Methodism 61
Mill, John Stuart 95, 203
Miller, Anne 206
Miller, Eric 208
Mitchell, Arnold 202
Monod, Jacques 201
Morris, William 66, 201

NATTA (Network for Alternative Technology and Technology Assessment) 207
Nader, Ralph 205
National Economic Development Council (NEDC) 140
National Health Service 26
National Council for Voluntary Organisations (NCVO) 152, 155
Nerfin, Marc 196
Newland, Kathleen 202
Nicholls, William and Dyson, William 208
Novarra, Virginia 87, 203

OPUS 197

Organisation for Economic Cooperation and Development (OECD) 152, 161–162
Owen, Robert 120

Pahl, Ray 208
Parker, Stanley 199
Perkin, Harold 198
Pilkingtons 158, 159
Planning Exchange 155
Pleck Community, Walsall 153
Polanyi, Karl 198
Policy Studies Institute 179, 186
Pritchard, Alison xiv
Pym, Denis 205

Rank Xerox 157, 158
Rights of Man 116, 118
Roberts, Keith 171, 206, 207
Rocky Mountain Institute 207
Rothwell, Sheila 196, 203
Rowbotham, Sheila 203
Royal Institute of Public Administration (RIPA) 186
Russell, Bertrand, 66, 201
Russell, Peter 202

Sahlins, Marshall 202
Sale, Kirkpatrick 201
Scarbrow, Ernie 115
School for Advanced Urban Studies 179
Schumacher, E. F. 199, 201
Scott, Hilda 208
Scottish Community Education Centre 152
Seabrook, Jeremy 122, 123, 204
Seattle, Chief 74
Shankland, Graeme 208
Shay, Paul E. 202

Sherman, Barrie 123
Shoard, Marion 199
Shorter, Edward 82, 198
Smith, Adam 23, 61, 91–97, 197, 203
Social Credit 172, 206
Social Democrats 140, 143
Spretnak, Charlene 205
Stacey, Nicholas 206
Stanford Research Institute (SRI) 76
Stonier, Tom 19, 197
Strathclyde Community Business Ltd. 155
Swann, Bob 204, 207

Tawney, R. H. 57, 60, 90, 200, 203
Taylorism 112
Teilhard de Chardin, Pierre 75, 201
Terkel, Studs 198
The Other Economic Summit (TOES) 203, 206
Theobald, Robert 206
Thompson, E. P. 109–111, 198, 200, 203
Tiger, Lionel and Fox, Robin 80, 202
Toogood, Philip 163, 206
Tories 137–138, 142

Town and Country Planning Association (TCPA) 164, 199
Trist, Eric 208
Trotsky 121
Turnbull, Shann 207
Turner, John 199
Turning Point 196

Universal Declaration of Human Rights 116, 118
URBED 151, 204

Voltaire 67
Volunteer Centre, the 152

Wainwright, Hilary 114, 203
Watts, Tony 163, 206
Weber, Max 56, 200
Whigs 137–138, 142
Wilde, Oscar 105
Wilson, Des 205
Woodbrooke College 196
Woolf, Virginia 81, 202
Work and Society 206

Yankelovich, Daniel 78, 202
Youth Call 206
Youth Training Scheme 160, 163

Subject Index

absentee worklords 36, 37
age of Aquarius 4
age of automation 4
agriculture 10, 174
another development 196
autonomy 119

banking collapse 135–136
banks 172
barefoot economists 74
building societies 134
Business As Usual – vision of
    the future 3–16, 39–51,
    67, 85, 129, 139

calling 57, 58, 61
capital 50–51, 128, 131–133,
    173
capitalism, 32
Cartesian split (qualitative/
    quantitative) 60, 72, 95
cash crops 37
cash flows 134–136, 174
centralisation 127, 128
communication age 4
co-operative self-reliance 109
co-operatives 153–154, 179
common ownership 153–154
community business 18, 152–
    155, 179
community land banks, c.l.
    trusts 177
consumer society 38
Corn Laws 141–142, 173

cosmogenesis 201
credit creation 171–172

debt 128
decolonising (the work/finance
    empire) 107, 136, 144–145
dependence,-cy 26, 30, 31, 35–
    38, 115–117, 119, 137, 178
divided society 15
division of labour 32, 35, 43,
    61, 92
do-it-yourself (DIY) 156

economic growth 8, 104
economic recovery 20
economics 89–91, 183–184 the
    'new economics' 183–184
economy 8
    black ec. 101, 168, 170
    dual ec. 100
    formal ec. 8, 15, 84, 86, 97,
        98, 100–102, 200
    four-sector ec. 17
    informal ec. 8, 15, 84, 86,
        97, 98, 100–102, 200
    local ec. 26–28, 35–37, 132–
        133, 152, 154–155, 160,
        177–179
education 11, 47, 163, 182–
    183, 207
effective demand 98
employees 15, 16, 19
employers 15, 156–159, 184–
    185

employment age 1, 28–38
employment relationship 19, 22, 23, 32
enabling policies 186
enclosures 31
energy 10, 40, 41
environment 42–44
equal opportunities 83
ethic
    job e. 64
    leisure e. 67
    resourcefulness e. 205
    usefulness e. 123
    work e. 25, 55–69
ethical investment 181–182

factors of production, political significance of 138
factory system 31
family 28, 31
feminisation of work 87–88
financial advice, need for 133
financial institutions 18, 19, 50–51, 127–136, 179, 184, 186–187
financial mumbo-jumbo 126
flexible work patterns 15, 23, 88, 130, 157, 187
food 10
fossil-fuel age 40
free market in labour (as a result of GBI) 168

government 137–145, 184–186
'green revolution' 41
gross national product (GNP) 104
guaranteed basic income (GBI) 25, 49–50, 130–131, 158, 166–173, 177, 178

HE (Hyper-Expansionist) – vision of the future 3–16, 39–51, 67, 86, 129–130, 139–140, 142

health 12
    holistic h. 75
household 18, 20, 26, 27, 28
'housewife, only a' 29
housing 9
humanistic psychology 199

impersonal (relationships, attitudes) 29, 31, 32, 39, 119, 127–129
incomes 7, 48–50, 127, 130, 131, 165
incomes policy 102–103
industrial age 4
industrial revolution 3, 71, 109, 124
industry 17, 156
inertia, academic, 184, managerial 185
information age 4
information industries 19
intrapreneur 157
investment 50–51, 132

job creation 161
job dissatisfaction 33
jobless growth 21
just price 89–91
just wage 101, 105

labour movement 109–125
labour-power 94
land 50, 96, 173–177
    land purchase 177
    land taxation 172, 174–177
    land tenure 177
Left, the post-industrial 123
leisure 9, 24–25, 44–47, 123, 182–183, 207
Leninist strategy 121
liberation of work xi 190
local currencies 179
local economy (see economy)
local enterprise, i.e. trusts 18, 20, 155, 159, 160, 179

local government 159–161

machine, nature as 71
  human bodies as 72
  planet Earth as 74
  society as 72
  universe as 72
mad scientist 15
manufacturing 14
market prices 98
masculine/feminine duality 79–81
matriarchal society 80
meaning of work 33, 64
medieval society 56, 62, 71, 73, 89–91, 126
men's work 31, 32, 81–88, 168
middle-class pioneers 69
monasteries, dissolution of 31, 135
monastic life 56–59
money 7, 29, 45, 46, 58, 59, 100, 103–104, 126–136
multinational companies 36, 37, 38
mutual aid 109

natural law 95
needs 98–99
neo-classical economists 97
neo-scarcity 78
newly industrialised nations 18
nuclear power, a dependency-creating technology 180

office automation 18
organisation development (OD) 184
ownwork x, 16, 20, 25–27, 41, 45, 46, 90, 124, 130–133, 149–188, 193–195
paradigm, p. shift 55, 191–192
part-time jobs 15, 23, 88, 130, 157, 187
patriarchal society 80

pension funds 134
personal change 5
planners, planning 9, 42, 164, 173
politics, politicians, political parties, p. alignments 137–145
possible futures 3–16
post-scarcity 78
poverty trap 166–167
practical skills 182–183
pre-industrial society 82, 83
pre-industrial work patterns 28, 35
productive labour 94, 95, 99
professions 184, 188
Protestant Reformation 56, 61, 71
puritan merchants, p. divines 57, 58, 59, 61

quality of working life (QWL) 184, 208

reformist strategies 120
Renaissance 71
research and development (R and D) 181
responsibilities 116–118
revolutionary strategies 120
rights 116–118, right to be responsible 118
robots 42
Russian revolution 120

savings 132
self-employment, s.-help, s.-reliance, s.-service, s.-sufficiency 13, 42
serfs, serfdom 30, 189
services, s. industries 14, 17, 18, 99, 139
'skunkworks' – see intrapreneur
SHE (Sane, Humane, Ecological) – vision of the

SHE (*cont.*)
  future 3–16, 39–51, 67, 78, 86, 130–132, 141, 142, 192
slavery, slaves, 23, 30, 189
social change 5
social entrepreneurs 151
social sciences 183–184
socially useful products 114–116
space 44, 45
space age 4
specialisation (also see division of labour) 32, 35, 43, 92
symbols of success 77
syndicalists 120

taxes (to finance GBI) 169–171
technology -ies 7, 32, 41–42, 156, 180
technology assessment 181
third world xi, 37, 85
time 45, 58, 59, 60, 158
trade unions, t.u. movement 109, 110
training 47, 182–183
transport 9, 42

unemployment – as the only alternative to employment 33, 34

unemployment centres 152, 179
utopian socialists 120
utopian: wishful thinking, fantasy 14, 15

value, values 13, 71, 76–79, 89–106
  capital values 135–136
  labour theory of value 91–97
  land values 174–176
  masculine/feminine values 79
  quantitative/qualitative values 100–105
  use value/exchange value 97
voluntary associations 152
voluntary simplicity 77
voluntary work 168

welfare state 26
women's work 31, 32, 81–88, 168
working class 61, 62, 63, 73, 109–125
working time 20, 23, 24, 158
worldview 55, 71, 73